To Be Frank

**BUILDING THE AMERICAN DREAM
IN BUSINESS AND LIFE**

Frank Morsani
With Dave Scheiber

BlackWood
BOOKS

Published by BlackWood Books

ISBN 978-0-692-52513-5

Front Cover Photography: Mike Sexton

Book Design: Susan Spangler
www.susanspangler.com

BlackWood
BOOKS

The small, long-living Blackwood tree, sometimes called the tree of music, is one of the most valuable heartwoods in the world. Its broad roots nourish the soil in which it grows.

The Blackwood tree's durability, density, and resistance to extremes of heat and humidity make it the ideal wood from which to craft wind instruments, whose surfaces can be burnished to a gloss so high that they reflect the light.

In similar ways, the Blackwood tree symbolizes Frank and Carol Morsani's strong commitment to supporting and nourishing the arts, health and education—bringing light to their community in ways that are deeply rooted in their shared values.

CONTENTS

I want to dedicate this book to my wife, Carol, who for 64 years has accompanied me on this journey. She has been by my side through tough times and good times. She has been an inspiration—her wisdom and support have been outstanding. We continue to give each other strength and happiness.

I would be remiss if I did not mention my co-author, Dave Scheiber, for his excellent writing and research. This has been a daunting task. Dave has been a pleasure to work with and I will always be grateful.

I also want to thank Joel Momberg for the encouragement to write this book. His friendship continues to be a great source of strength and understanding.

Last, but not least, I want to thank the hundreds of employees who have worked with me—and for me—for these many years. I hope I aided them in their life's work and that their lives have been shaped for the better by our association.

I clearly remember the first time I met Frank Morsani.

He was at the top of my list to call when I became the CEO of the University of South Florida Foundation in 2008. He was one of the university's largest and most engaged donors—and, surprisingly, Frank wasn't even an alumnus of USF. I couldn't wait to meet him and find out more.

When he stepped into my office, I was absolutely in awe. I had felt that royalty had entered the room. Not royalty with pomp and circumstance—not exclusionary royalty—not royalty with any pretense or airs. This was true royalty. If I believed in "auras," I'm sure I would have seen a serene royal blue or a Roman Empire purple framing the top of his head.

Actually, the top of his head was snow white and his face well-tanned and smiling. He was soft-spoken and looked at you as if you were the most important person in the world. That was just one of his many talents. He was interested in everyone and everything. And when he addressed you, you felt important.

This man—this icon of our community—was actually interested in what I had to say.

In our first meeting he was full of questions. These weren't random questions, by the way.

Frank Morsani is someone who does his homework. He had researched me. After all, if I was the one ultimately in charge of his philanthropic treasures, he wanted to be sure I was the right fit.

My questions all took a back seat. He didn't want to know about my professional career. He was too smart for that. He could get that information anywhere. He asked about my family, where I grew up, what my father did, my philosophy of life. He would later share that when he interviewed applicants for management jobs in any of his numerous businesses, he asked similar questions. He was much more interested in how they would fit in, how they interacted with people and what kind of family they came from.

I remember just staring at the man thinking—"this guy sued Major League Baseball—and won!" Every once in a while, he would throw in a story or two about his own life, his wonderful wife Carol and his thoughts about the university.

When I asked him about his philanthropic philosophy, he shared his unique life goal. I never forgot it:

"You know, the way I see it is that we live our life in thirds. In the first third—we learn. That's when we get our education from books and in life. The second third—we earn. We work and invest and live our lives. And in the final third—we return. Carol and I are in the final third. We are returning our treasures to those we care about."

In the pages that follow, you will read about these three stages in detail. Frank Morsani is a man who lives life fully ... every day. He works hard and "gives" hard. He even fits in a little golf now and then.

You'll also see that all three stages have a little overlap.

While Frank was learning, he was also earning. He worked his whole life. You might say that was part of his learning process as well. Prior to delving into the automobile business, Frank was a craftsman, a tinkerer and a mechanic. The machines and engines he worked on mirrored his life—most were set on full throttle. Frank is still working every day. He is still buying dealerships, learning about cutting edge technology, advising business professionals, and speaking to and mentoring students. His "returning" hasn't slowed either. In the Tampa Bay area, it's hard to travel far in any direction and not see the Morsani name on a building or a business Frank hasn't touched.

And throughout most of his adult life he has done it all with the love of his life, Carol Morsani. Her strength, her tenacity and her wit have complemented Frank's personality, making them truly one of the most dynamic couples in the Tampa Bay area.

The Carol Morsani Hall at the Straz Center. The Frank and Carol Morsani Clinic. The Morsani College of Medicine—those are just some of the places that bear their names from Florida to Oklahoma, where they grew up and attended Oklahoma State University. Frank and Carol often say that they shy away from the recognition and would be happier if their names were not on buildings … but they understand the need. Their names inspire others to do the same. Their names stand as a seal of excellence and a valued resource for others who wish to invest.

I truly have been blessed by having the opportunity to know the Morsanis and write my thoughts in this book. If you ever have a chance to meet Frank, he'll remember you. He will remember something that made you special to him in his mind.

Everything he has accomplished—everything that has inspired others to emulate him and everything he has been to me—is what truly makes him so special to all of us.

Joel Momberg
Chief Executive Officer
The University of South Florida Foundation

Frank Morsani is the model of how business leaders and their families can make a real difference in their communities.

Throughout my business career, Frank has been one of my role models for making a difference in the community. As someone who is well respected as a business leader, he has shared his success generously during his life, with charities involved in education, healthcare, culture and support for the poor.

I had the good fortune to work with him on the Dali Museum Board. Frank donated his business management and leadership skills as well as financial assistance. Moreover, he demonstrated great interpersonal skill and was a pleasure to work with in the process.

I've witnessed his largesse at the University of South Florida, the Tampa Bay Performing Arts Center and in other organizations, too many to mention, that make Tampa Bay a better place to live and work. I salute Frank and Carol for all that they have done for the community and the impact that they've had on me.

Thomas A. James
Chairman of Raymond James Financial, Inc.

For many years, the life I've been so fortunate to lead has been chronicled in scrapbook after scrapbook, each one meticulously assembled by my wonderful wife Carol. The old newspaper clippings and glossy photographs tell endless stories of the distinctive stops along the way in business, family life, politics, sports and philanthropy.

I treasure these bulky keepsakes and the way they transport me back in time to experiences and events that helped shape the person I am.

They hold memories that make me proud—of building a thriving nationwide automotive business, working alongside three U.S. presidents on public policy and helping educational, medical and cultural institutions grow through the fulfilling philanthropic work Carol and I have undertaken. And they carry recollections that remain difficult for me to revisit, tied to my all-out pursuit of a Major League Baseball team for the Tampa Bay area and the personal and legal struggle that ensued.

Now my journey moves from the pages of scrapbooks on my shelf to the chapters of this book. It is a reflection of the course I have followed from the lean years of my childhood in the Great Depression of the 1930s through all of the satisfying endeavors that still engage me today—from philanthropic projects with Carol to my work on expanding new, more affordable forms of automobile fuel with compressed natural gas.

In between, I've learned valuable lessons about life, business and leadership and had more than my share of memorable adventures, so many of them with Carol at my side.

Several years ago, I stated in an interview that I wanted to write a book about my experiences, entwining the people and events that taught me so much at each turn. I'm excited to have made that wish a reality and that you hold in your hands a copy of the end result, To Be Frank: Building the American Dream in Business and Life.

I gave a lot of thought to why I wanted to write this book. First and foremost, I hope that you—the reader—will be able to apply some of the knowledge that I've gleaned along the way to your own life. I have strived to imbue everything I do with integrity, to treat people with respect and work as hard as possible to achieve a desired outcome. Following those guidelines doesn't guarantee success, but you'll be able to look yourself in the mirror each day no matter what—and keep pushing on to the next challenge.

In addition, I hope you'll see from reading my life story that adversity need not deter you from reaching a goal, but instead can give you the strength to achieve it. That has been the case for me, and it can be the same for you. From my earliest years, my life has been filled with challenges. There was the tiny Arkansas home with no running water or electricity I lived in as a child; the many odd jobs I juggled before I was 10 years old to bring in money for my family; and the collegiate night classes I took in economics and statistics, while traveling five days a week as a master car mechanic for the Ford Motor Company. Learning to cope with and conquer hardship was as vital a part of my education as formal academic training. I like to say that overcoming adversity is the hallmark of success, whether in our personal or business lives.

Many of the stories and experiences you will read about in these pages illustrate the tenacity passed down to me from my parents and grandparents, fueling an inner confidence and abiding faith in my ability to find solutions to problems and to clear the hurdles that may block the path ahead. I urge you to examine these examples of persevering through challenges and setbacks and see how they may apply to your own experience.

Adversity is a fact of life, so be prepared to accept the inevitability of trouble looming on the horizon. How you tackle it can make the crucial difference in determining your course. Remember this: We learn from our failures and disappointments every bit as much as our successes, and sometimes more.

When our daughters, Leann and Suzy, were youngsters, we moved around the country quite often as my automotive dealership career unfolded. It wasn't easy for them, but Carol and I always stressed looking ahead to new opportunities rather than lamenting what was fading in the rear-view mirror. When we moved from Fort Lauderdale to the Philadelphia area, we talked about moving to the land that gave birth to the U.S. Constitution and the pleasure we would have investigating that together. When we drove cross-country from New Jersey to Southern California, we focused on the fun of living near the glitz and glamor of Hollywood. The point is, we always tried to remove the negatives and dwell on the positives, taking advantage of every new situation and set of circumstances.

In 1955, I was working as a welder on a pipeline in New York and was fired—simply for being Italian. Later, when my dealerships began to grow and prosper in Tampa, there were whispers in some corners that I must have had Mafia backing or I couldn't possibly have achieved what I did. If they only knew how much money I had to borrow to get my start in business, and the countless hours of hard work creating opportunities.

That's another lesson I hope you'll take away as you read on. Always be alert to new opportunities and be ready to take advantage of them. Should a promising door open, be prepared to walk through. So many people in the world are hesitant to do so, but there can be great rewards waiting on the other side. As you'll see later in these pages, the gears of my mind are constantly turning in search of new and better ways of doing things—and I've been open to entrepreneurial endeavors that held potential for success.

There is one fundamental point I want to convey to collegians and young professionals who read this book: The American Dream is alive and well. I've been fortunate to take advantage of it, and you can, too—using every experience as a lesson to build on, relentlessly pursuing your passion whatever it may be, remaining constantly hungry to read and expand your knowledge, and finding a way to make a difference.

In the pages that follow, you'll not only follow the narrative flow of my life but gain an understanding of how the foundation and guiding principles of my management philosophy and leadership style emerged. You will see how I developed a decentralized approach to running my dealerships, trusting my employees to do their jobs without being micromanaged—an approach that has given me the flexibility and time to pursue so many other rewarding ventures. And you will learn, among other things, about my four essential pillars for creating a highly motivated staff and a successful business, whatever it may be. See how these apply to you in your work life, as either a manager or employee—and consider whether these principles suggest any adjustments or new directions you may need to take.

I hope they will help you move forward in your own business and life challenges.

So now we begin. The road ahead winds through the landscape of a lifetime, marked by rewarding experiences, remarkable individuals and resiliency. I'm appreciative and humbled that you have decided to travel it with me.

Frank Morsani
2015

CHAPTER ONE

Working for a Better Life

You might say that my story begins in a sleepy nook of south-eastern Arkansas, near the tree-lined banks of the Mississippi and the river's winding path from Memphis to New Orleans. This is where two dusty stretches of asphalt meet—Highway 65 running north to Pine Bluff and Route 82 rolling east-west across the state—and where a little-known piece of American and Italian history converges. It can be found in the delta town of Lake Village, resting on the shoreline of a placid ribbon of water that curls off the Mississippi called Lake Chicot. It's a part of the world that holds countless tales—a place where Spanish explorer Hernando de Soto traded furs with a friendly Native American tribe led by Chief Chicot, where Confederate troops clashed with Union soldiers in "The Engagement of Old River Lake" during the Civil War and legendary aviator Charles Lindbergh completed his first night flight in 1923. And for a young couple from Italy, it represented the glowing promise of a near utopian existence.

My paternal grandparents, Emedio and Adele Morsani, emigrated from the ancient northern Italian town of Aviano to Lake Village just before the dawn of the 20th Century. They were driven by a determination to make a better life through their hard work, resilience and a spirit of adventure—traits that would be passed on to my father and one day become part of my own DNA.

In the late 1800s, they were like any of the thousands upon thousands of European immigrants who pursued new hopes and dreams as they arrived at Ellis Island in the shadow of the Statue of Liberty. But unlike the vast majority that settled heavily in the northeastern United States, they and a small group of fellow Italians pinned their future and that of their families to a stretch of land some 1,200 miles to the southwest of New York City. The reason for this migration toward the nation's heartland lay in a fertile area of Lake Village called Sunnyside Plantation. A New York banker and entrepreneur, Austin Corbin, purchased the cotton and sugarcane plantation in 1886 and, ten years later, signed an agreement with the mayor of Rome, Italy. The pact brought some 1,000 individuals from central and northern Italy to work at Sunnyside with the expectation of steady work, owning their own property and thriving in the land of untold opportunity.

My father's parents arrived in 1898, seeking to leave behind the hardships of home. But Corbin and his partners had turned to Italy merely as a means of finding inexpensive labor to work the plantation. Unfortunately, the contingent of starry-eyed Italians innocently had signed a deal that would require them to work for 22 years before they could become landowners themselves. They were unaware that Corbin and his company controlled virtually every important business in town, making it impossible for them ever to get out of debt—let alone think about acquiring any of their own acreage.

The scam Corbin and his colleagues perpetrated eventually came to light, prompting the federal government to intervene on the immigrants' behalf. But by then, the utopian dream was already unraveling amid failing crops, a malaria epidemic and settlers deciding to pursue work elsewhere in the state or beyond. A number of Italian families relocated to the Ozark

Mountain region of northern Arkansas, feeling more at home in a climate that was closer to the one they had left behind in Italy. They named their new settlement Tontitown, after Henry de Tonti, the Italian explorer who roamed the lower Mississippi Valley in the late 17th century. Their first efforts at creating a cash crop in apples failed when disease killed the trees, but the settlers had grape vines sent from back home and they took root—laying the groundwork for flourishing wine vineyards and even a Welch's Grape Juice Company plant in the 1920s.

My grandfather Emedio, a master carpenter back home in Italy, and grandmother Adele were among the families that relocated to Tontitown, and earned a living growing Concord grapes. In time, they moved into a tiny home on a patch of farmland, just as they had dreamed. This was the simple life my father, Amerigo, was born into. He never got out of the sixth grade—in that era, you had to put in long, hard hours at home to help support the family. But I say without hesitation that he was one of the most successful men I have ever known. He always worked tirelessly to provide for his family and held the opinion that you went where the jobs were—a philosophy I would adopt years later.

Tontitown was a tiny, tightly knit community, well-known for its grape festival every August and numerous church functions—the perfect kind of gathering for two teens to meet and fall in love, as was the case with my father and a young girl from town named Helen Crane who'd caught his eye. They married in 1926—when he was 19 and she just 16. A year later, they had their first child, a daughter, followed by the deep sadness of an infant son who died in utero. At the same time, my father felt a keen sense of responsibility to support his young family. And his first order of business was to get a job. Coming from his farming background, he never had the luxury of developing a marketable or formal skill. But he had heard there were jobs to the north in Detroit—not in the manufacturing plants but with the railroads, which transported new auto-mobiles to cities across the country. He was a naturally skilled craftsman and promptly got hired to construct the mechanism that would hold the autos safely inside the rail cars. I suppose that made my father the first Morsani to start in the car business, long before I gave it a try.

From there, he became a welder. This was not a lucrative Depression-era occupation—in fact, it paid exactly one dollar per day. But the steady work allowed my parents to purchase a little home in Brighton, Michigan, which is where I was born in 1931 and my brother followed a year later. We lived as well as a growing family could on next to nothing, but my dad's meager income wasn't enough to stave off the inevitable. In 1934, with the economy spiraling in the grip of the Great Depression, my family—like so many other working-class Americans—lost our home. It was gone almost overnight. The only viable option, spurred by desperation, was to return to Arkansas and move in with my mother's parents. While I don't remember anything about the time in Michigan, I recall this phase of life in Arkansas quite vividly.

I remember the sadness hovering over our crowded household when my grandmother passed away in 1936, and how I started grade school at age 6 a year later. And I remember that my mother had two brothers, who were a bit on the rambunctious side. During the 1930s, they rode the railroad cars throughout the Southwest—Arizona and New Mexico—working in the fruit and vegetable fields to earn a living. I recall that periodically they'd get tossed in jail for causing trouble—shooting out streetlights or getting into scuffles—and my grandfather would have to scrape up enough money to travel to whatever town they were in out West and bail them out. My mother would get so upset when the boys, who made no secret of their love of the bottle, would return from another stint riding the rails. Counting my grandparents, parents, their three young children and my mom's two wayward brothers, there were nine of us squeezed into a no-frills, two-bedroom house.

In other words, it was a classic portrait of Dust Bowl life in Depression Era America. Our home had no electricity, no indoor plumbing or any of what you would consider basic amenities—unless you count the hand-cranked telephone that allowed us to make sporadic calls into town. I'll never forget the day the house was fitted for electricity. It was a huge undertaking for the power company to lay the line, because the ground in that part of Arkansas was like granite. The workmen needed dynamite to blast holes for the utility poles. Until then, we had to use kerosene lamps for light. For drinking water, we relied on a well dug into the back yard, lowering a bucket to bring up enough water to fill our needs for the day. That's how we also got our water for bathing, which was done outside in a galvanized tub when weather permitted.

In spite of the constant difficulties we faced, this was the life we knew and we felt fortunate to have a roof over our heads, food to eat and an abiding sense of optimism that we'd make it through. We had a loving family, though not one that showed it in a demonstrative way. We didn't dwell on worry, though there was certainly no shortage of concerns to go around back then. We all just knew that we had to do whatever it took to get through a day, a week or a year.

My grandparents and parents often reminded us that a lot of people had a much harder time than we did. Our little house faced west and had a cozy front porch that we could gather on in the evenings, plus two more side porches facing south and north. The kitchen was cramped but functional. It adjoined a small living room, next to a bedroom. To make room for the whole family, my grandfather, dad and uncles finished the attic, converting it into a large bedroom. Grandma and grandpa slept in the bedroom downstairs, and the rest of us piled into the attic. Meals were noisy but full of life—with cuisine heavy on possum, or whatever game was out there that we could shoot. My grandparents raised a few cows for milk and one we eventually had to use for beef. For dessert, you could always count on persimmon pudding being served due to an abundance of persimmon trees—I ate so much that to this day I can't bear the thought of tasting that fruit.

But as I said, we were in better shape than a lot of folks. In those Depression years of 1936-38, men would quietly walk the dirt road in front of our house on a quest for food or a few pennies to buy a cup of coffee—a disheartening march you could see almost anywhere across the United States during this period. The scene was particularly prevalent in the poorer states such as Arkansas and Mississippi but a common sight throughout the Dust Bowl states of the nation's south and mid-section as well. No men ever traveled together, just one at a time trudging down the road or along designated alleys in the city. I recall how they would come around back—never the front—and knock on the screen door. Despite being dirty and tired, they were complete gentlemen, politely asking, "Ma'am, do you have something I could eat?"

My mother or grandma always found something for those famished men. I found it interesting that they never came to the front door to beg for food; there was a certain dignity and respect to the way they approached us and others, and an understanding on the part of the women that these men needed a helping hand. It was a way of conveying compas-sionately that we were all in this together, and that generosity of spirit is something that made a strong impression on me. It also instilled in me a strong sense of wanting to do the right thing. What my grandmother and mother did for those suffer-ing men, in such dire circumstances, was absolutely the right thing to do.

As a child, I did whatever I could to help as well. That meant getting my first job at age 9, earning spare change in town shining shoes at a barbershop. It was at this time that we moved to Oklahoma, leaving behind farm life and moving 100 miles to the west into a small home outside the bustling city of Tulsa. I branched out with a paper route, delivering the Tulsa World early in the morning before school, and going door-to-door in the afternoons to deliver such magazines as the Saturday Evening Post and Ladies' Home Journal or do my best to sell subscriptions. By 10, I also found time to pump gas for a dime an hour—enough to pay for a loaf of bread at the time, so it was a great deal for a kid wanting to pull his weight. There wasn't a lot of time for playing around, though I did build a makeshift car for a soapbox derby once, using the engine from an old washing machine—perhaps a precursor to my future in the automobile dealership business. I always did well in school, though I would much rather have been thinking about ways to earn money than about math or homework in general.

Every Sunday, we went to church as a family—a tradition that no doubt strengthened our resolve for the week and workload that lay ahead. That's also where I learned about tithing. As a youngster, I always put two or three pennies into the collection basket—following what I had seen as a basic principle of giving to others, even when you yourself had barely anything to give. We were taught that our acts of generosity and faith would be rewarded, so we didn't hesitate.

This was our life and we accepted it. We never thought about how difficult it was, or wallowed in pity. We had enough to get by and thought we were fine. At the same time, my father wanted to make life better any way he could. That meant he was increasingly gone a lot, getting into pipeline construction in the late 1930s—a job that suited his skillset as a welder and meticulous craftsman. Living near Tulsa, known then as the oil capital of the world, Daddy was right in the heart of the action –major oil companies like Texaco, Philips 66, Continental and

City Service had home offices in the region. That's where you lived in order to get the work, and my father got plenty of it.

He would leave around Easter time, as soon as the weather was favorable, and stay on the road—working the pipeline that stretched across the nation—until the snowy winter months made the work too tough. He would be home with us perhaps four or five months out of the year and the rest of the time Mother was home alone, caring for the children. She was a very independent woman and I believe that influenced each one of us to be independent, to trust our instincts. Later on as we became young adults, she wasn't sure we should all be so independent, but that's another story.

My mom came from the same kind of solid stock that my father did. My maternal grandfather, a man named Charlie Crane, oversaw the sprawling Crane and Lamer ranch that ran 35 miles from Cleveland, Oklahoma to Tulsa. He and his father, along with his two brothers, ran this ranch, which was actually located in Oklahoma's Indian Territory. In fact, my aunt was the first white child born in Indian Territory and my momma was born there, too—in a sod hut. My grandfather took part in the Cherokee Strip Land Run of 1893, with more than 100,000 people trying to claim land in what would become the nation's 46th state in 1907. He homesteaded just outside of Tulsa and started the town of Bristow with its very own post office, so the ranchers could get their mail. Bristow's still there today—a testament to my grandfather Charlie Crane's vision and fortitude. It often strikes me how each side of my family is so interesting and so different. But what they shared in common was an uncommonly strong work ethic.

My mother exemplified that. She ran the household and raised the kids often on her own, and never failed to make sure we all did our chores and schoolwork. And that solid foundation allowed my father to leave for long stretches of work without having to worry about anything on the homefront.

He was a tremendously skilled laborer who could make virtually anything. If he walked into a room, he would turn over an ornate chair to see how it was built. And he'd say, "I think I can make that." No wonder that every pipeline contractor wanted my father to work for him—and he worked in that field until he was 62. That is hard work. You're forced to lie on your back, and start at the top and weld your way around to the bottom. One of the jobs on the pipeline was known as "tying in to a hot line" and they'd fly him to Canada or all over the States just to make one weld.

He was a good man—on and off the job. Because he had a name that not all of his co-workers could pronounce, Amerigo soon became Elmer. But there was no confusion about his talent level. At a certain point, my dad was called upon to actually build pumping stations along the pipeline. His boss would tell him to get the materials he needed and go build a station, simple as that. He could read a blueprint and would go out to the site with nothing but a pile of pipes and joints scattered all over the place. And my father, with his sixth-grade education, would put it all together. There's no doubt he inherited the carpentry and craftsman gene passed on from his father and relatives from Italy. But his fellow workers enjoyed being on jobs with him for more than his extraordinary ability. He was always calm and gentle. He never created any issues. He never drank, other than maybe a glass of wine here or there. He'd report for work early, leave late and do a wonderful job in between. And above all, in this challenging economic chapter of our country's history, he was a tremendous provider for his family.

He was equally kind as a father, so naturally I relished the opportunity to go out with him and work on the pipelines when I turned 13—we didn't have labor laws then, or at least they were pretty lax. I'd join him on jobs during the summer and started learning the ropes as a "welder's helper."

Dad would weld a piece of pipe on the back of a truck to show me how it was done, and during delays or slow moments, I'd go back there and practice what we called "running beads." I truly enjoyed learning how things were made, and that passion soon coincided with my work at home on the farm with all the equipment required to plant and harvest.

In 1945, my dad decided the time was right to get a bigger farm. Having grown up on one, he felt comfortable with everything it took to make a successful farming operation. And he liked the idea of being able to come back from his eight-month stints on the pipeline to raise cows and crops and fortify our finances. If times turned bad again, he knew we would be able to feed and care for ourselves this way. He had earned enough money working pipelines to purchase two farms—a 260-acre spread that we lived on and a smaller one of 140 acres some eight miles away. And shortly after the end of World War II, in May 1946, we were back living the country life.

It had only been six years since we'd resided on a farm so the surroundings were very familiar to me. At 14, much of the extra load fell to me as oldest male child and I welcomed the responsibility and trust he showed in me while he was off working the pipelines. Sometimes my younger brother helped, but I was the one in charge of keeping things running. We raised cattle, oats, wheat and corn and did that all the way through my high school years, from 1946 through 1949. We'd wake up in the pre-dawn hours to milk our five cows, fill up the five-gallon milk cans and place them out front. They'd be picked up and taken to a pasteurizing facility, and from there delivered to customers living in the city. Then I'd make a mile-and-a-quarter walk to catch the bus to school and come straight home late in the afternoon to do whatever work was needed on the two farms.

Somehow, I managed to get my homework done in between the farm work and still have enough energy to get through the school day. Working the farm provided an advanced education in its own right: You learned how to fix just about anything, because there wasn't enough money to pay somebody else to do it. It certainly helped to be mechanically inclined, and fortunately my dad's innate ability with his hands was passed on to me. We used to joke, "Give me some baling wire and we'll make it work."

Looking back, I never really had much of a childhood. But I never thought about that at the time. You simply did what you had to in order to get by—no different from how life had been when we all squeezed into my grandparents' home in Arkansas during those dire years. I never had time to play any organized sports at school—and fielding an athletic team at the school was difficult anyway, considering there were only 17 students combined in the sophomore, junior and senior classes. I essentially fell right into the role of an adult. But I never felt envious of other kids who had more time for recreation or relaxation. And I certainly never felt as if we had a bad life because of the daily rigors we faced—far from it. The way I look at it is that we had a great life. I have no regrets about any aspect of my early years, because that created the foundation of my value system later in life.

Our lack of material possessions never defined our happiness as a family or as individuals. Even on the new farm, we had no running water and no telephone, though thankfully we did have electricity by then. Looking back, I'm also grateful for the calm, steady manner my dad passed on to me during that time. Oh, I can lose my temper or get upset like anybody, but on balance I tend to be more even-keeled like my father. That characteristic served me well solving this problem or that on the farm. That's when the roots of my managerial style took hold as well. When I was 14 or 15, I ran a crew with 10 or 12 men working for me all summer, baling hay to make money all over the region. I was basically the foreman, and I learned how to hire good people. It didn't matter to them that I was half their age—they needed the work. I also hired some boys my own age because they had to make money for their families. I paid them and made sure they did their jobs well.

One side benefit of this rugged lifestyle is that it made me physically strong, capable of handling heavy lifting and long hours of labor with no issues. I didn't have a problem until the second semester of my senior year during gym class at Ramona High School. I suffered a strained arch, making it impossible to walk to the bus stop. There was no car to reliably transport me to school. So my mother made a big decision, one that certainly showed her faith in my ability to adapt and be independent. She arranged for me to finish out the semester in the busy capital city of Tulsa, about 40 miles to the south. The move to an urban setting would allow me to have a short, manageable walk to my new school, Will Rogers High. I had no family or friends to stay with so the only option was to rent a room in a home near the school.

It wasn't easy to make such an abrupt switch at that point in my high school career. But you did what you had to do, not what you wanted to do. There was no other choice except to try to make the best of a difficult situation. And one day, sitting in Mrs. Gibson's English class, my circumstances took a turn for the better. I noticed a pretty girl at a desk nearby and, when the moment was right, I made a point of introducing myself.

Her name was Carol Walsh. I liked her sense of humor and the sparkle in her eyes and she seemed to think I was okay, though she didn't show an abundance of interest. Years later, Carol admitted that she'd been hearing about me from former junior high school classmates of mine who'd gone to high school with her—and though other girls were talking up the new guy in school, she wasn't particularly impressed by what she had heard. But as it happened, the Junior-Senior Prom was approaching and, being a newcomer, I had no date. So I got my courage up as the dance grew closer and asked Carol if she'd go with me. It was the best decision I ever made, even though it took some time—and amazing timing—for destiny to run its course.

CHAPTER TWO

The Tale of a Pickup Truck, a Buick and an Aircraft Carrier

The 1949 Junior-Senior Prom at Will Rogers High was certainly a more elaborate affair than any school soirée I'd ever attended. The dance had the upperclassmen talking for weeks. It was booked at the popular Mayo Hotel in downtown Tulsa—an ornate, 14-floor building of brown brick and white stone completed in 1925 and the tallest building in all of Oklahoma at the time. The Mayo had ceiling fans in each of the 600 rooms to offset the steamy heat of summer, and boasted the distinction of being the city's first hotel to offer running ice water. Larger-than-life celebrities booked their stays at the towering, palatial hotel during visits to town—people like Charles Lindbergh, Babe Ruth and Charlie Chaplin. So naturally we were looking forward to being special guests ourselves inside the Mayo's lavish ballroom come prom night.

When the big evening arrived, I pulled up to Carol's pleasant suburban house in the old Ford pickup truck that I'd driven on endless errands between our two farms.

This was apparently a good move—not the pickup truck, but the fact that I'd arrived, as promised, to personally escort Carol to the dance. It seems that her previous prom date had kept her waiting and waiting. He had gone straight to the prom and expected to meet her there, a decision that didn't go over well with either Carol or her father, an ex-Marine now working as an oil company accountant. I scored points with him right away by showing up in a timely manner. Being a farm boy somewhat out of my element, I wasn't quite sure what kind of impression I'd made, but Carol said her father liked me, even though he wouldn't admit it. Apparently, as I learned years later, her dad enjoyed teasing her by referring to me as Tony because of my Italian heritage, and got a kick out of playing a Hank Williams song on the family Victrola—a tune entitled Tennessee Border, which included the line, "I picked her up in a pickup truck / And she broke this heart of mine." If he kidded like that, it meant you were okay in his book.

Despite my success with the pickup, I don't remember much about the dance itself. Somebody spun records with pre-rock 'n' roll hits of the day—like Vaughn Monroe's Riders In the Sky, Frankie Laine's Mule Train and Perry Como's Some Enchanted Evening. I wouldn't say it was an enchanted evening but I enjoyed chatting and dancing with Carol. I also had a spontaneous idea of how to commemorate our date: At the end of the party, we sneaked a silver spoon out of the Mayo—and both had a good laugh about it.

Now, from the way it sounds, you might expect that this was the first of many dates in the months to come. But the truth is, our first night out was almost our last. I can't explain it other than to say my life was so intensely busy—finishing up high school, returning home to run the farms during the summer and preparing for my first semester at Oklahoma Agricultural and Mechanical (later to become Oklahoma State University)—that there was no time for a budding romance. I was completely focused on the work and priorities that faced me on a daily basis. I simply never followed up with Carol, who was left to think, "I don't know if he's slow or if I was boring."

I went off to Oklahoma A&M in Stillwater in late summer—following the lead of my older sister Patricia, who'd attended the University of Tulsa—with hopes of expanding my horizons beyond farm life and pipeline work. From the start, I poured myself into school with classes in mechanics and engineering. My parents had no money to send me to college, of course. To get through, I constantly had to work when I wasn't in class, holding two or three jobs for several hours a day to pay for books and tuition. In addition, it was too expensive to live on campus, so I had to rent a small room in a family's home. I had a part-time job as a gardener for the university, while working at a campus drug store and even the school library. The pay was minimal: 35 cents an hour. But those 35 cents made a big difference if you managed to work 15 to 20 hours a week.

Somehow, despite the steady grind, I managed to get my homework done, attend classes and squeeze in a few hours of sleep at night. And then, it happened. During the spring of my second semester that freshman year in 1950, I was standing on a campus street corner when a car drove by and honked at me. There were two smiling young women inside and one of them was waving from the passenger window. I instantly recognized her as Carol. I'd never imagined that our paths would cross again, but in that sudden twist of fate, here she was. I waved back and watched the car drive down the street, with the image of my pretty prom date playing on my mind the rest of the day.

Carol, as it turns out, wasn't exactly swooning at the chance sighting of me on the street corner: "I thought, 'Hey, I know that boy. It's Frank Morsani, my old prom date." And though she didn't give me much more thought in the aftermath, I did some digging and confirmed that Carol was a student at the university. What's more, I found a phone number for her and called her the next day. Fortunately, Carol was understanding enough to give me another opportunity to take her out and we began dating regularly after that. Carol was an interior design student and we were both very serious about our studies. But we enjoyed each other's company and grew closer through the rest of the spring. Our budding relationship was interrupted that summer because of my pipeline work with my father and the need to help my mother on the farm. But when school began again that fall, we happily resumed seeing one another. But soon, I felt another kind of pull that would present a new challenge to us.

Several months earlier, in June 1950, the United States had been drawn into the Korean War. By September, as Carol and I began our sophomore classes, General Douglas MacArthur conducted an amphibious landing known as Operation Chromite on the city of Inchon, retaking Seoul from North Korea and moving north as fighting raged on. I was keenly aware of these events and found myself at something of a crossroads, pondering my next move in life. Not long before, my fellow Oklahoma A&M classmates and I had taken a series of tests, followed by an interview with a psychologist—all designed to help us zero in on a post-college career. The recommendation for me: I should return to the farm to live and work. That was the last thing I wanted to do. Instead, fueled by a sense of duty to our country and desire to chart a new course, I decided to join the Navy.

Even though I was 19, I had to have parental permission to take that serious step. My mother was completely against it, not only worried for my safety but also aware of her dependency on me to run the farm in my dad's absence. She refused to give her blessing, but my father did—and on Oct. 24, 1950, I officially enlisted.

The truth is, I very likely would have been drafted eventually had I not joined. If Carol was worried, she didn't let it show. And since she was from the city, I'm sure the notion of one day living and working on a farm held no appeal to her whatsoever. She supported my decision to sign up. We were young, adventurous and had a sense that everything would turn out just fine.

The Navy appealed to me more than the Army primarily because I didn't particularly like the idea of fighting in a fox-hole—clean sheets sounded far more comfortable. In short order, I was sent to San Diego for 12 weeks of boot camp. It was definitely an exhausting experience, but my years of hard, physical work had prepared me well for the rigors we endured. Though I didn't dwell on the likelihood that some of us might not make it back from wherever we were heading, it was im-possible not to consider one's mortality—and future—at a time like this. Carol and I hadn't had enough time together to give our relationship a chance to flourish. In some ways, we were just starting to build a foundation. But I knew there was a spark that could grow into something special. I'm not sure of the precise moment when the idea came to me, but in the spirit of simply taking life as it came in this time of uncertainty, I decided I would ask Carol to marry me.

There wasn't much time to act. I bought a simple engage-ment ring in San Diego with the meager earnings I'd accrued, wrapped it in a small box and addressed it to Carol in Okla-homa. Then, I hand-wrote a letter to her laying out my feel-ings in a marriage proposal. I realized it was a different type of approach, but these were different times—requiring creativ-ity and a helping hand from the U.S. Postal Service. I made sure to write that she would be receiving a box containing a surprise—and not to open it until she had read my letter. Then I mailed the letter to Carol, waited a day, and mailed the engagement ring.

I imagined the look of surprise on Carol's face when she got that letter, given that we hadn't discussed the idea of mar-riage in the first place. What I didn't imagine was that the letter would get lost in the enormous shuffle of mail from the base—or in transit back east—and arrive three or four days after Carol received the box with the ring. Fortunately, she didn't need a letter to figure out what my intentions were, though she likes to joke that "I engaged myself" when the ring arrived with no explanation. When we were finally able to talk by telephone, Carol said "yes"—to my delight and relief. She confessed she was surprised because she really didn't suspect that I had marriage on my mind. Carol, in fact, was still adjusting to an emotional upheaval in her life—her father had died of a heart attack that winter and she'd left college to offer her mother support. To hear her tell it, her dad would have been none too happy about my proposal to his daughter, either: "He was not eager to have his daughters get married, and particularly that young! You didn't mess with his girls."

We may have been engaged, but considerable obstacles needed to be surmounted to make the wedding happen before I shipped out. For one thing, a man couldn't get married in Oklahoma before the age of 21 without parental consent. We were both 19, and my mother initially wanted nothing to do with any wedding talk. I'm sure she had envisioned me eventually returning home from the war to settle into running the farm. My joining the Navy was bad enough—but a wedding that might ultimately take me away from the farm was too much.

Suffice it to say, my mother had no fondness for Carol at that point and no intention of signing her name to a wedding consent form. So, as he did with my Naval enlistment document, my father stepped in and signed the paperwork allowing us to proceed with the ceremony. I had a much-anticipated, two-week leave after completing boot camp before reporting to my ship—the aircraft carrier USS Antietam (CV36), named after one of the Civil War's bloodiest episodes, the Battle of Antietam, fought along Antietam Creek in Sharpsburg, Maryland. The Antietam was docked in Hunter's Point just outside of San Francisco. And there was plenty of time to get back home to Oklahoma, marry Carol and return in time for my new assignment. But things didn't exactly go as smoothly as I had planned. Far from it.

My main priority was busing it back home to Tulsa with all due haste and I gladly left wedding preparations to Carol, her sister Bev and their mom. They planned the ceremony for the front room of their house, the same place Bev was married. But this plan did not strike my mother, who by now had reconciled herself to the fact that I was indeed getting married, as a good idea. If there was going to be a wedding, she felt strongly that it should be in a church. So the location was switched to the First Methodist Church in Tulsa, where Carol and her family attended.

We were married in a simple ceremony on February 9, 1951. My brother served as my best man, Carol's sister was the matron of honor and a handful of other family members and friends attended. It went off without a hitch, but we were both aware of an air of tension between our mothers hovering over the small reception that followed at Carol's house. Neither of us felt like eating due to the stress, compounded by an extremely tight schedule to get back to San Francisco and my new assignment on the Antietam.

We hopped into a two-door gray 1950 Buick we had purchased from Carol's mother—a car that her father had owned only several months before passing away, and one that her mother didn't need because she couldn't drive. This was his first Buick after always buying Chevrolets and he was proud of that two-door, torpedo-back car. It was typical of bare-boned vehicles back then—with a radio, standard transmission and no air conditioning, but we were happy to have our own transportation back to northern California—even though the trunk was so cramped we could barely fit any of our belongings inside. There was just enough time to get to Oklahoma City, where we stayed overnight at Bev's apartment before making a beeline for the West Coast.

The drive was one long blur of road signs and tail lights, as we barreled non-stop to Northern California. I remember how unbearably hot the days were with no air conditioning in the car and how tense it was to share the twisting roadways with the speeding semi-trucks at night. But I also remember cuddling in the front seat, with my right arm around Carol, letting her hold the steering wheel as we barreled along Route 66, sharing our new road in life.

We arrived in San Francisco with only days to spare before I had to report for duty. Right away, we rented an apartment in Alameda, about a block from the water. The place provided easy access to the Alameda Naval Air Station and Hunter's Point, where the Antietam was docked—and I'd get to the ship each morning via a landing craft that transported us across San Francisco Bay.

Our apartment was a cramped one-room unit with a bedroom, little kitchen and small bathroom. We had no sofa, but there were two mattresses, so we rolled one of them in half and tied it together to create a couch. And, of course, refrigerators were a luxury item back then. Instead, we had what was fittingly dubbed an "ice box" to preserve our perishables. When our block of ice melted, we'd put a sign in the window for the ice man. He'd see it, then trudge up the stairs lugging a new 25-pound chunk of ice on his back. As Carol recalls, "You had to remember to empty the pan, but you'd forget sometimes—and the water would leak. One time, the woman below us started banging on her ceiling with a broom stick, because we'd forgotten to empty the pan and the water was leaking into her home!"

I'll never forget the first meal Carol made for us—fried chicken, mashed potatoes and peas, using her mother's Sunday dinner recipe—and canned peaches for dessert.

Finally, the morning to report arrived. My job was to help with the restoration of the Antietam, a massive, 27,100-ton ship that had been commissioned in 1945, too late to see active combat in World War II. For several years, it sat in mothballs and was officially decommissioned in 1949—only to be recommissioned a year later for the Korean War and designated as an attack carrier.

When I reported for duty, there was an enormous amount of work to do to get ready for action. There were only about 150 of us at that point, though we'd eventually ship out with 3,400. That's where my background on the pipeline suddenly came in handy—thanks to my father and the experience I had gained since my early teens, I knew how to weld. That's a particularly good skill to have when your workplace is made of steel. I told the division officer that I could help with any welding that needed to be done, so just like that—I became the ship's welder.

The doctors or those in charge of the galley on the ship always needed something fixed in the infirmary or kitchen, so I would go down there and weld it for them. The benefit of that was that I never needed to make appointments to see a doctor. I'd get help on the spot if I had a problem. And I never had to go to the mess hall to eat—they'd bring the food up to me, wherever I was. In addition, a little welding ingenuity enhanced our menu selections on a regular basis.

We were housed in the back end of the ship—the fantail—and that's where the trash was dumped overboard at night. In the military, food was not allowed to be kept overnight, to cut down on the chance of contamination and potential cases of food poisoning. As a result, each night all the uneaten food was carried back to the fantail area in big garbage containers. Some of that untouched food was much tastier fare that had been intended for officers in the ward room.

What a shame, we thought, to see all that delectable cuisine go to waste. This called for some creativity. In short, we decided to build false bottoms into some of these big garbage containers. Then, certain pals in the mess hall—grateful for all the welding we'd regularly do for them—carefully stashed uneaten officer's cuisine in the bottom portion of the containers and concealed the meals beneath a moveable tops section that held actual garbage. The plan worked like a charm. When we lifted these tops off, we had our own special menu of officer-quality items inside the false bottom, as opposed to the powdered eggs and milk that would otherwise have awaited us in the galley.

That was only part of the surreptitious culinary operation. A few of us cut a small hole into a steel wall of our shop below the flight deck. That proved to be a perfect storage area to secretly hold some of the purloined food originally destined for the officers, not us seamen. There was even a drain in one of the storage areas we'd devised, so we were actually able to weld a pipe into place and create a working sink, too! From time to time, we added a jolt to our grapefruit juice by mixing in the alcohol from the torpedoes, sprinkling in some salt and enjoying a "torpedo juice" cocktail. The ship's captain conducted regular inspections but he never found our own private locker in the side of the ship.

Our inventive shenanigans made the long, grueling days a bit more tolerable. I guess you could say that thanks to my welding ability, my medical needs and appetite were taken care of quite well—and I didn't have to wait in any lines.

Early on, we spent much of each day loading munitions aboard the Antietam, and sometimes would go out to sea for practice runs that lasted several days or weeks at a time. But quite often I was able to return home to the apartment at the end of the day to spend time with Carol, who was still struggling to adjust to the upheaval in our lives.

It didn't take long for her to realize a change of routine was needed, so she decided to find a job to minimize the pervasive loneliness. Not only that, we needed the extra income since we were splitting my modest $90 a month pay from the Navy— $40 for me, $50 for Carol. She had no trouble landing work, starting out at a business called Dorfman Hat Company, typing invoices. That didn't last long and she found another job in San Francisco through an employment agency, typing and doing office work for a nice man named Mr. Biagini (whom she mistakenly called Mr. Baganini the first day, but he didn't seem to notice). Prospective employers were often wary of hiring sailors' wives, concerned that they'd spend time training the women, only to suddenly lose them when their husbands were transferred.

You'd often see signs outside homes around town that underscored how low enlisted men were regarded—"Sailors and Dogs Keep Off the Lawn"—largely due to the ones who got rowdy in bars. The reality was that the ones causing the most problems were with the U.S. Merchant Marine, not the Navy. These Merchant Marine sailors were a rough-and-tumble bunch in that period, but we were all lumped together in the minds of many folks in town. In today's world, you can't even imagine anyone in the military receiving such harsh admonishments, but in base towns at that time, sailors were persona non grata.

Fortunately, Mr. Biagini was so impressed with Carol that he eventually offered her a fulltime position. Staying busy worked wonders in helping to take Carol's mind off of her feeling of isolation so early in our marriage. Unlike today, there were no support groups for military wives. They were completely on their own. But our challenges were not unique to us—it was simply the way things were back then.

There was less time to wonder about what might lay ahead once our ship sailed across the Pacific Ocean and into hostile waters off of China. We knew that brutal warfare was already intensifying in Korea, but both Carol and I felt a sense of confidence that I would make it home safely. Maybe our blind faith stemmed from being young and naïve. Whatever the case, we were more concerned about being separated long-term than about the notion that something might happen to me. It was a hard moment for both of us when the time came to ship out from Hunter's Point. Carol and I said our goodbyes on the dock and then I boarded along with several thousand fellow seamen and officers. Many crowded on the deck and waved to loved ones as the refurbished carrier churned through the San Francisco Harbor and off to face the unknown of war.

There was no turning back as the dock faded in the distance. With a mixture of fear and adrenaline, we knew there was a job to do. And as a young man who'd been working hard one way or another since childhood, I was ready to do mine.

CHAPTER THREE

To War and Back

Churning through the Pacific waves in February 1951, we could have been preoccupied by fear—conjuring up brutal images of warfare during the days and nights aboard our new water-bound home. Our new reality was underscored by the daily sight from the flight deck of periscopes trailing us as we reached the Sea of Japan. They were attached to the Soviet submarines that tracked our every move and were a sign of the growing Cold War tensions between the U.S. and Soviet Union. Many of us had graduated high school only a year earlier and had dreamed of far different futures—pursuing college educations, careers, romance and other familiar possibilities. Instead, nearly a decade after the Japanese attack on Pearl Harbor that thrust America into World War II—back when most of us hadn't even reached our 10th birthdays—we were on our way to fight an ominous enemy in a distant part of the world.

But at 19 or 20 years of age, you don't look at it that way. You're driven by a youthful sense of invincibility and adventure and you don't dwell on the danger of an assignment—you just do it. That's how I saw my new role as a young Navy seaman heading into a combat zone. I'd learned to look at life that way from an early age, growing up not knowing how my family would get by in an era when so many Americans struggled to survive. We just did what needed to be done each day—pulled together, worked hard at whatever jobs needed to be done and had faith that everything would turn out for the better.

As it happened, the landmark Battle of Chipyong-ni unfolded during the month of our deployment. It was a decisive victory for the United Nations forces, led by the U.S. 23rd Infantry Regiment against units of the Chinese People's Volunteer Army. The action helped drive the larger Chinese Army back in a major triumph for the Eighth Army—a victory that would eventually turn the tide of the war. Yet, aboard the Antietam, we were insulated from the daily developments of war and much too busy to think about anything but tackling our unrelenting workload.

In my case, that meant working long hours as a welder, with an official classification of aviation hydraulic mechanic and responsibilities for repairing planes and getting them ready to return to battle. Patching bullet holes, making sure rivets were done just right and fabricating other necessary repairs, I realized how much I had learned from watching my father, with his talent for fixing things. Each day, our planes flew back to the ship from their missions over Korea, often badly damaged and requiring endless patching and fixing—work that often meant teaching myself a new skill. Our division was called Ship's Company. We weren't assigned to squadrons or maintenance crews, and that term—Ship's Company—reflected our strong sense of connection to the entire mission we were carrying out.

Inheriting a touch of my father's ingenuity wasn't the only thing that came in handy at this time—so did my summers helping him on the pipeline. It turned out that, like my father, a Lieutenant Commander of the Antietam had worked on pipeline jobs in and around Oklahoma, as a superintendent. He didn't know my father, but the fact that I had done pipeline work myself established a connection between us, even though it was taboo for enlisted men to associate with officers.

I didn't correspond much with my father or mother while I was overseas to tell them about any of this. I wrote to Carol often, describing the jobs we performed, but I spared her some of the details that I knew would cause concern and I made sure she knew how much I missed her.

The most frightening things we saw were the fires aboard the ship, especially serious because we were on an aircraft carrier. They were a constant hazard and could be devastating. To understand the problem, you need to picture an aircraft carrier, with planes being launched into flight by catapults. As one group takes off, the next moves to the front of the deck to be fired into action, leaving room in back for the incoming planes to land. When planes return to the ship and prepare to touch down, you hope and pray that the pilot doesn't make a mistake. But mistakes happen—and there were some terrible collisions with incoming aircraft hitting the planes lined up in front of them. Talk about an unimaginable type of fire, compounded by jet fuel leaking everywhere, with flames sweeping over the deck and thick black smoke billowing skyward from an orange-yellow inferno.

We had what were known as "duty stations" during landings, and because of the potential for devastating accidents, it was essential that you stay at your assigned station. My station was on a catwalk, some 60-70 feet above the hangar deck. We had compartments up there protecting stores of ammunition from exploding when planes crashed below. On one particular day, a pilot misjudged his landing, rammed into a line of planes and ignited a horrific explosion. I could feel the gasoline from the deck on my skin. Everywhere I looked, fires raged below me, and we had run out of foam needed to extinguish the flames. Along with another enlisted man, I grabbed a fire hose and began blasting water at the flames. That was a mistake—using water on a gasoline fire only spreads the fire. Fortunately, an officer named Lieutenant Baker saw that we were in danger of getting badly burned, and aimed a hose filled with foam at us from below. That was the scariest moment I experienced on the ship. To add to the potential disaster, we were standing right next to the huge ammo room. At any moment, if things had gotten out of control, it could have blown up.

We lost 10 pilots during our tour. Though we were spared some of the horrors of war experienced by ground troops, I was occasionally sent up on the flight deck to help retrieve the bodies of airmen who died in crashes. The images are forever etched in my memory. I will always remember one pilot with his hand still grasping the control stick, his skull in his helmet and his face no longer there. That's when the reality of war truly hit home.

I did my best to put scenes of that kind out of my mind. It was part of war, and you had no choice but to learn to deal with whatever happened. And I've learned that any life experience, even the most difficult, can teach us valuable lessons. Looking back, I see many ways in which my Navy career helped lay the foundation of my future in management. One fundamental lesson I learned: pass responsibility to the lowest common denominator. By this I mean that every employee, no matter what their position is in the organization, has individual responsibility for meeting the standards of his assigned job—a system that strengthens the entire operation and makes it function most effectively. Now fast forward to running an automobile dealership many years later, when I applied that principle of organization. One example: I expect the person who cleans the cars to take responsibility for purchasing supplies needed to do the job. The general manager doesn't do that, nor does the service manager. The people in charge of cleaning the cars know what they need—so let them buy the supplies.

Another lesson that stuck with me was to volunteer for just about everything. You will learn a number of things that will benefit you at some point in your life. I followed that philosophy throughout my time on the ship. If a sign went up calling for volunteers, I'd step up. Invariably, I'd wind up learning something I didn't know and broaden my horizons. You may not think of it that way at the time, but there's a good chance you'll end up being glad you did. The military can be boring if you don't take steps to try to make it more interesting—and boredom creates problems.

I've always just liked to be involved in many different things. I learned early on the importance of keeping your mind alert and ready for new opportunities or ways to improve what you're already doing. In the military, I was suddenly put in charge of people—in some cases, supervising men who had more stripes on their sleeves than I did. I relate my ability to handle that responsibility to my teenage years of baling hay on the farm, when I gained experience managing men older than myself. Apparently, my Navy superiors recognized an innate leadership ability in me, and gradually entrusted me with responsibility for overseeing others, in spite of differences in age and rank.

Soon after coming home, I was sent to an experimental Navy squadron named VX5. There were two of them: One was stationed at the Patuxent River in Maryland, the other in Mountain View, California, where I went to work. I had already absorbed a lot of knowledge about airplanes, and was excited about the opportunity the Navy now offered me to learn more.

While I was working with the squadron, I enrolled in a two-year program at San Jose State University, taking night courses and earning certification as an airframes and hydraulics mechanic. I knew at some point soon I'd be leaving the military and this seemed like a good way to prepare for a civilian career that fit my abilities and interests. I would now be certified to work with airframes and hydraulics, though not with engines.

In the midst of the VX5 program, while earning my certification, I was placed in charge of a section of highly impressive men in the squadron. The pilots were extremely bright, with doctoral degrees in engineering. The group was tasked with engineering and designing a method for dropping atomic bombs from fighter planes, as a way of providing support for ground troops. The tactic was termed "toss bombing," and involved these elements: planes to carry bombs, other planes to identify targets, and planes to determine when to drop the bombs. In modern combat, it is all computerized. But, at that time, there were questions about how to make the process work successfully—and our job was to figure out a way, conducting tests with water bombs.

Initially, our plans called for the pilots to fly 500 feet off the deck and veer straight up in the air—anywhere from 12,000 to 15,000 feet—and eject an atomic bomb in a pinpoint arc designed to hit its target. The pilot, traveling straight up, would then steer the plane onto its back and move safely out of range before the bomb detonated. Without such a plan, a pilot could be killed by the devastating blast below. The blueprints for that type of test were meticulously worked out in our northern California base at Moffett Field in Mountain View, with actual tests conducted in a secluded spot to the south in the western Mojave Desert. The area was and is home to the Naval Air Weapons Station at China Lake, covering most of the Navy's land for weapons and armaments research. My team was not involved with the mathematical and technical plans. We maintained the airplanes to ensure that the tests would be conducted successfully, and dropping water bombs assured that our tests and measurements would be as accurate as possible. On occasion, we'd be asked to do such experimental things as add fins to the 500-pound bombs to see how they might affect the operation.

Our work also included travel to different parts of the country to stage air shows that demonstrated how the "toss bombing"—among other maneuvers—would work. One of the events was a major gathering held in the Washington, D.C. area. Our group—myself included—flew to the nation's capital to put on a private exhibition for select members of the Senate, House of Representatives, the Supreme Court and President Dwight Eisenhower. With such a distinguished crowd of onlookers, we wanted the military operations we were showcasing to be picture perfect. The event was held in Quantico, Virginia, with special bleachers set up for V.I.P. spectators to take in the impressive display. President Eisenhower was not in attendance but he sent officials from the administration in his place. They all arrived on charter busses, along with members of Congress, and were ready to observe precision bombing of makeshift targets that had been set up—from a comfortably safe distance.

A speaker was installed so our guests could listen in to the conversation between the tower and the pilots. The planes were scheduled to take off from a location along the nearby Patuxent River, where I was based for the proceedings. One of my jobs in preparation for the event was to help create 500-pound bombs called "The Shapes," painted Day-Glo orange so they could be easily seen from a distance as they were ejected from the jets. Several of us sat inside an airplane back at the Patuxent airstrip listening to the show unfold and we observed, with satisfaction, that everything was working with pinpoint precision. We could hear the P.A. announcer explain to the audience how the entire operation worked. He says, "Here they go," and soon after adds, "You can see them coming in and how the pilot is flying his pattern, and now he's ejecting the bomb. Now you see how he's flown safely away and how those bombs are coming."

There was a momentary pause in the announcer's play-by-play, and then his voice suddenly boomed over the P.A. at the site—and through the radio speakers by the Patuxent.

"THOSE DAMN THINGS ARE GONNA HIT US!!"

Somehow, the buses had been accidentally identified as targets and several of them bore the brunt of the 500-pound payload. Nobody was injured, thankfully, because the crowd was all seated a good distance away. But I can remember listening to the radio and thinking, "What in the world went wrong?!" Being physically away from the site, our hearts sank during the momentary commotion. But mistakes do happen. Suffice it to say, the airshow abruptly ended and everyone on hand was driven back to D.C. and the Pentagon. I can laugh about it now, but at the time there was most definitely no humor to be found in that unexpected outcome.

For the most part, though, the work we did in developing "toss-bombing" and other aerial innovations went very well. And I was a lucky young man to be part of the program, coming right on the heels of my service in Korea on the U.S.S. Antietam. There was—and still is—a massive hangar at Moffett Field, the length of a football field but much taller than a stadium and big enough to house a blimp. That is where, over a period of two years, they literally built the first VTOL—Vertical Takeoff and Landing airplane—and flew it inside the hangar.

The huge scaffolding needed to construct that plane, designed to take off and land vertically and then transition to level flight, was a sight to behold. There were wheels on the vertical stabilizers and wings to hold the VTOL in place, and the craft featured a turboprop engine driving contra-rotating propellers. The ambitious project was akin to erecting a skyscraper inside a building. And talk about noisy! After the initial test, they brought the plane out of the hangar for a test-flight, tethering it to keep it under control as it took off vertically, powered by the turboprop. There's a new, multi-billion-dollar airplane you may have read about today, the F-35, which does the same thing we were experimenting with long ago with different engineering. We were pretty far ahead of the curve. The whole experience was amazing and I consider myself fortunate to have been part of it.

This period marked a major change in my life after my eight months overseas. Carol and I had rented a small apartment in Mountain View and had always wanted to start a family. Soon, the news came that we were hoping for: Carol was pregnant. I looked forward to being a father and I knew Carol would be a fine mother.

Everything progressed in seemingly routine fashion, but a measles outbreak began to infect many families on the base. As a child, Carol had the disease but this was a new strain of the measles. In 1953, we didn't know how serious an illness it was. I remember that Carol went to the base hospital when she noticed spots showing up on her body, but the doctor told her, "You've got so many freckles I don't see any spots." So he sent her home, without diagnosing her case of the measles.

There were no sonograms or ways of detecting problems in utero. And sadly, we didn't know that a problem had begun to undermine the pregnancy. Doctors did not notice any irregularities until she was eight months into the pregnancy, when they could no longer detect a heartbeat. Carol had to go though the trauma of delivering our baby stillborn. The loss left us both with a feeling of emptiness, but all we could do amid the unexpected adversity was to accept what happened and push forward. Little by little, life began to regain a sense of normalcy. While I attended school at San Jose State and worked in the VX5 program, Carol found an office job at

Stanford Research Institute. And we began focusing on what our next step would be.

In 1954, I had the opportunity to re-enlist with the Navy and continue on the path I'd been following in aviation. Though I enjoyed the cutting-edge work and learning about aviation, Carol and I had decided to return to Oklahoma. I had been seriously considering returning to pipeline work along with farming. I was experienced in working with Caterpillar and International Harvester equipment and pictured myself going to work for those companies someday. So I passed on re-upping with the Navy in September 1954 and we headed home to re-enroll at Oklahoma A&M. The G.I. Bill paid us $90 a month to go toward the cost of college, but we still had to figure out a way to pay for living expenses in Stillwater. That meant finding odd jobs when I went back to school and started to attend classes.

There was no financial support available to us from our family. It was never even discussed. But neither of us worried about how things would work out. Just as I'd grown up with a strong feeling that we would make it through despite our hardships, and held that same conviction when I sailed off to war, I felt confident that we would succeed in this new chapter of our lives—no matter how much work I'd have to do.

It turns out I had to do even more than I ever imagined.

CHAPTER FOUR

Driven To Succeed

The long haul back to Oklahoma to start a new chapter of our lives, picking up where we had left off before the Korean War, was fueled by a high-octane blend of exhilaration and anticipation. I was well aware of the enormous amount of work that lay ahead as I endeavored to start a new career away from the Navy and aviation. We'd only been gone from the state for four years but it seemed like twice as long, having packed so many life experiences into that timeframe. We'd left home under so much pressure—my leaving for combat, followed by the stressful whirlwind of our wedding—that it felt good to have a chance to make a fresh start with so many possibilities on the open road before us.

But I couldn't resume college right away. I left the Navy on August 24, 1954 and the first semester at Oklahoma A&M had already begun. I figured it wouldn't hurt to earn money to create a modest cushion for us to live on, so I found a job as a mechanic at Tulsa Air working on planes and kept it until early January 1955. I began classes in the winter/spring semester and my course load mirrored my unbridled enthusiasm and motivation. Once I was back on campus, I was determined to push myself as much as I could to make up for the time I'd been away from school. I chose classes in trade and industrial education, which equates in today's world to industrial management.

During the time I had spent time in Japan while in the Navy, observing the country's culture and the determination of its people, I'd fallen in love with Asia. World War II had only been over for some six years, but I was deeply impressed by the Japanese citizens' work ethic, which I'd observed while I was in Tokyo re-supplying the ship. They were hungry but they worked hard to get by in terrible conditions. That truly resonated with me, and lay behind my decision to minor in Far Eastern History—another step in my lifelong pattern of turning potential detours or negatives into learning opportunities and personal growth. I had learned so much in the Navy simply by volunteering for any assignment that came along. At the time, I was probably just bored and wanted a change in my daily routine, but volunteering for duty was a way to keep my mind active, to continue my education and learn about things I never would have otherwise encountered. My friends on the ship gave me a hard time—they thought I was trying to curry favor with the officers. That wasn't true at all. I just wanted to stay busy—the same way I am to this day—and expand my horizons with new challenges. When classes started, all of those efforts contributed to making me a better, more rounded student.

My schedule was filled with 27 hours of classes a semester—about 12-15 more than needed—with 7 a.m. classes six days a week. On top of that, I took on a handful of side jobs just as I'd done in my first go-round in college. I worked as a mechanic in Stillwater, starting the shift after my Monday-through-Friday classes ended at 2 p.m. I'd fix cars until 6 o'clock and then begin my night job as a cab driver, doing countless pickups and drop-offs until 10 or 11 p.m.

Oklahoma was a dry state at this time, but there was no shortage of bootleggers in town who made sure that anyone who wanted alcohol could get it. That led to my side education in the fine art of what was known as "pitching pints." The bootleggers would call the cab company, and I'd drive to wherever they happened to be, pick up the liquor and deliver it to a happy customer waiting at another location. The customer paid me, and I'd go back and pay the bootlegger. And meanwhile, as Carol has reminded me, she was home doing my homework.

I had a mountain of assignments, and Carol made sure they were always finished. She read the books that I didn't have time for, did the outlines and made sure everything was always ready to turn in on time. Granted, our system is not what I would ever recommend to any student as a means of getting through college. But these were unusual times and required a creative solution for keeping me ahead of the curve. Carol did such a phenomenal job, in fact, that a professor I had years later used one of the outlines she devised for me to teach one of his classes—without knowing it was her handiwork.

As you can imagine, there was no chance of ever getting to bed early with all the work bearing down on us. I had to wake up well before dawn in order to get to the campus in time for those 7 a.m. classes. I rode my bicycle so that Carol could drive our car to an office job she'd landed at the university. She'd hurry home at night to make a quick dinner for us and take care of whatever work I'd left her. My electrical engineering teacher clearly was wise to our system, though. He cut out a comic strip one day and stuck it in my folder—it depicted a professor telling a student, "Your wife is a wonderful typist." Carol did indeed type all of my papers and did it immaculately—and he clearly knew what was going on. But I believe, too, that he appreciated how seriously I took his class and how driven I was to succeed, even if my success required an invaluable helping hand.

In a way, you could say this was the beginning of the team approach Carol and I have taken throughout our lives. She had more than enough to keep her busy in her own right, with the campus office job, followed by a secretarial position in town at the Methodist Church. Then, in 1956, life took a new turn when Carol gave birth to our daughter, Leann. We lived in a small, family-oriented neighborhood and one of our friends saw us leave for the hospital in the middle of the night. By the time I got home in the morning, everybody already knew that Leann had arrived.

As a new father, I wanted to get a handle on my crazy schedule, so I made the decision to give up driving a taxi at night and picked up some extra hours instead at the university bookstore. The job allowed me to get my books free, another big plus. But giving up the taxi job didn't alter the fact that I essentially worked my entire time in college. I can't argue with Carol's assessment: "Frank's always worked—he never really had a childhood, when he could go out like other kids and play until the street lights came on and it was time for dinner." I didn't see it that way. I just did what was expected of me in those challenging times. That was life as I knew it.

In May of 1957, the same year the college changed its name to Oklahoma State University, I graduated with a Bachelor's Degree in Industrial Education. In August, I earned Associate's Degrees in Automotive Technology and Service Management and another AA in Diesel Technology and Stationary Engines. Those two trade degrees teach you, in essence, how to fix things and how to run a shop, skills that certainly came in handy down the line. All told, I graduated with 160 hours, about 40 more than a typical B.A. requires. I was so hungry to learn and put myself on a path toward a rewarding career that it never felt like too much—even though looking back, it's clear that it was a daunting load, to say the least.

Oklahoma State truly provided me with an outstanding foundation for my future success in business and life. I've always said that a good student can get a good education anywhere. So many people think that unless you've gone to Harvard, Yale or one of the traditionally elite schools in the country, you haven't gotten a good education. But there are plenty of institutions of higher learning in this country that are top-notch. Oklahoma State gave me a superb education as a generalist, allowing me to apply the knowledge I gained in a variety of subjects. I still remember a class I took in conference leading. I learned techniques having to do with encouraging participation and recognizing nuances of body language—and I've put them to effective use countless times in life.

As I mentioned previously, my ambition at the time was to find a job with one of the two companies that manufactured heavy-duty farm and construction equipment, Caterpillar or International Harvester. I was familiar with their products and believed I would enjoy being part of the team that designed rugged new engines and machines. Still, I wrote to many prospective employers, including the big three automobile manufacturers—Ford, Chrysler and General Motors—and any company that made products with wheels, for that matter. I even contacted train manufacturers. My credentials coming out of college were enough to get me interviews in Detroit with Ford and Chrysler. I came away feeling good about each session and hoped that one of the companies would come through with an offer. To my surprise and delight, both of them did.

It was a tough decision between Ford and Chrysler, but Ford offered a training program that sounded intriguing. I didn't know at the time that Ford's former vice president of the international program had graduated from Oklahoma A&M, and his parents lived in Stillwater. But what I later learned was that

Ford hired many college graduates from Oklahoma, Texas and Kansas—and still does—due to the high quality of the technical education offered at these institutions.

In July, I made my choice and headed to Detroit for my first position—as a technical writer for the Ford Motor Company. Carol and Leann went to live with her mother while I immersed myself in the new job. I had always worked on writing well in school and my bosses were confident of my ability to create the tech manuals for new automobiles. I was placed in a select group of 400 people in Ford's national training program. Then, one day the company suddenly eliminated almost everyone, and I found myself in an even more select group—one of 10 who survived the massive cut.

I continued writing owner's manuals, an experience that gave me a chance to compare the manuals of that era with those produced today. In my opinion, today's manuals are inadequately written and don't fulfill their purpose. We were instructed to write the text for readers who were at a ninth grade education level. In my opinion, today's manuals are aimed at an MBA level—clearly why so many people don't know how to operate the equipment in their cars.

In addition to the owner's manuals, we wrote the service repair manuals for mechanics, explaining how to overhaul an automatic transmission or engine. We also were tasked with writing what are called labor and time schedules, something a dealer uses in order to know what to charge a customer—based on how much time a given repair should take. For instance, if an alternator goes out, we determined in our schedule that the repair should take an hour and 10 minutes. Those types of guidelines are still utilized today.

I can't help but think that some of my father's knack for fixing and building things was flowing through my blood when it came to excelling at this first job in the automotive business. It just came to me naturally. We had to take countless photographs of the internal workings of the car's engine, transmission and wiring, and compose instructions explaining how to disassemble or reassemble the components. Today you have computers to produce those graphics, but back then we would wind up with our photos laying all over the room. We did everything by hand—probably equivalent to the way Disney animators meticulously hand-drew scenes compared to the computer-generated imagery of today. Using our system, we certainly learned how to explain things well—a great skill to have in any line of work.

After completing my stint as a tech writer, I was transferred to Jacksonville, Florida, where Ford put me to work in a job that was a logical extension of everything I'd done in Detroit: training mechanics. Carol and the baby joined me there during a particularly cold, non-tropical type of winter in December of '57. We rented a house in Jacksonville, but the frigid weather made living conditions miserable.

Poor Carol—she'd heard we were moving to Florida and instantly envisioned balmy breezes, bright sunshine and relaxing on the beach. But this was—and still is—one of the coldest Florida winters on record, causing widespread destruction of crops and even killing cattle. Carol certainly won't forget it: "It wasn't cold enough to kill the roaches, and they were huge. It was so cold that Leann and I had to live in the hallway, wrapped in blankets on the floor. There wasn't enough heat to keep us warm, other than a kerosene heater that didn't help much."

But thankfully the weather warmed up soon enough and we began to settle in and began to appreciate the change of scenery. I was making an attractive salary for a young man with a growing family: $90 a week, totaling about $400 a month, or $4,800 a year. My college classes in engines and cars, coupled with the tech-writing experience, were part of the evolutionary process leading to this new opportunity: in charge of training Lincoln-Mercury mechanics throughout northern Florida and southern Georgia. I devised tests to ensure that they were qualified to work on our full range of vehicles, and traveled to dealerships in the region five days a week, amassing 60,000 miles per year. Sometimes, to be more time-efficient, I'd invite dealers from surrounding areas to send mechanics to whatever location I was scheduled to visit.

In one instance, I conducted a training-school session in Jacksonville, drawing mechanics from such rural Georgia areas as Statesboro, Waycross and Brunswick to a week-long program about automatic transmissions. Bear in mind that automatic transmissions were new and virtually unknown in 1957 and 1958. I had an array of beautiful schematics provided by the company and was very eager to bring the mechanics in attendance up to speed on new ways to get their jobs done. Using graphics definitely beat the alternative instructional method: hauling around a real transmission in my station wagon from dealership to dealership, using it as a hands-on teaching tool. A policeman had actually pulled me over one evening after noticing that the underbelly of my car was riding abnormally low to the road. He suspected I was a bootlegger delivering a heavy load of illegal liquor, until I explained what was causing my car to sag suspiciously—the extra transmission, plus my tools and anything else I needed to teach my mechanics.

I began my first lecture at my one-week transmission program Monday morning, explaining that I'd be giving little quizzes along the way to make sure everyone was absorbing the material. During a break at 10 a.m., one mechanic approached me.

"Can I speak to you privately, Mr. Morsani?" he asked.

It struck me momentarily funny that he called me Mr. Morsani, since I was only 28 years old. But I told him to share whatever was on his mind.

"These tests—I'm a good mechanic, but I can't read. And there are other men in here, too, who can't read or write."

I told him quietly not to worry; that I'd take care of it without drawing attention to their situation. This was a wonderful leadership lesson for me: never assume anything, as I had done simply taking for granted that all these trained mechanics had received basic education. And—when the situation calls for it— be compassionate and understanding. I gave these men tests, but instead of written exams, I critiqued how well they worked on the transmissions. And I spent a little extra time with them in those hands-on sessions, giving them whatever additional help they needed.

My role with Ford during this time required that I be a master mechanic. Very few mechanics were skilled at fixing air conditioning back then because it was so new. But I had to learn to be an AC expert, holding classes all over my territory. The reality is that we didn't have any technical training to speak of then in the state of Florida—in fact, very little such training existed in the South. There was a program at Louisiana Tech, but nothing like it in Georgia, Alabama, Mississippi or Florida. The reason for this, plain and simple, was segregation. The officials who had the power to create these programs declined to do so because it might cause minorities, specifically blacks, to take jobs away from white workers. It's not all that different from our immigration policy today.

In Florida, only two schools offered any programs related to automobiles: a private school in Miami and an institution in Jacksonville. Automobiles were becoming complicated, and not enough mechanics knew how to work on them—or simply knew how autos worked. Many were still operating with a Model-T mindset. Things were changing rapidly and I felt it was essential to increase our skilled labor work force.

Where I grew up, technical training had always been taught as a trade, and I'd earned two associate degrees in Oklahoma in the very field I was trying to teach now. But things were different in the deep south, in Florida and Georgia, and the serious shortage of skilled mechanics motivated me to start a program to teach the necessary skills.

My first step was to obtain permission to start a class for mechanics at St. Petersburg Junior College (now St. Petersburg College), but before that program got under way, Florida passed new legislation that propelled me in a different direction. In 1958, technical training—by law—was added to the curriculum of public high schools, and school boards were instructed to hire the necessary teachers.

The new law inspired me to take new steps. My job with Ford brought me in touch with a Lincoln-Mercury dealer in Tallahassee, who also happened to be the city's mayor. He and I talked frequently about improving technical education in the state, and our discussions led to the next step—exploring the topic with the governor, LeRoy Collins, a man later praised as the first southern governor to work toward desegregation in the South. Our discussions led to a plan for action: to create a tech program at Florida State University, educating high school teachers throughout the state.

I approached Ford about sponsoring a 30-day or 60-day program at the university for accrediting teachers in the technical arts—and I would organize the program and serve as head instructor. The response was an enthusiastic "yes." When I returned to Jacksonville, I proposed that Ford help out by lending automatic transmissions, air conditioners and other necessary components. Again, the company was completely on board with the idea, agreeing to provide anything we would need to educate the first class of teachers about servicing automobiles. At the same time, officials from Florida State contacted schools throughout the state, inviting teachers to attend. We felt we were on the verge of orchestrating a tangible change in creating a new wave of auto repairmen.

But much to my dismay and surprise, only one school in the entire state agreed to have one of their teachers participate in the program. Long story short: The grand plan to raise the level of technical training in Florida fell completely flat. The lack of response may partially have been related to the fact that the profession, in many places, had not progressed beyond bare-bone, dirt-floor operations and simply didn't strike a chord with enough people. Yet I firmly believe, as sad a commentary on society as it was, that a deep-seated reluctance still existed in school districts across the state to support a program that would inevitably raise the level of training for blacks—thus allowing them to compete with whites in the job market.

It wasn't long after this disappointing episode that Ford promoted me from service school instructor to service representative. My primary duty in this new role involved working with dealers on broader business issues. I continued to train mechanics in select situations but not nearly as frequently. Instead, this job—requiring me to be away from home five days a week—involved dealing more directly with consumer complaints, profit margins, gross earnings, determining car inventories, and issues of that nature. One of the challenging dynamics was that I was still under 30, giving advice to dealers who were 50 or older on how to do a better job of running their business. Though the age difference created some inherent friction, I found that by talking to people openly and honestly, and always with respect, my input was accepted. I think they came to respect me, in return, because a lot of them were having trouble solving their problems and I was a good problem-solver.

The truth is, most of them had gotten their experience as used car dealers who received automobile franchises after World War II. Few of these men had earned a college education, and a fair number hadn't even finished high school. But when they came out of the service in the mid-1940s, they were handed dealerships from General Motors, Ford or Chrysler and—presto—opened a car lot. Consider this: At that time, the

United States had a population of 100 million, with only three giant manufacturers and roughly 50,000 dealers throughout the country. Today, with a multitude of manufacturers, the number of dealers has dropped to some 19,000 nationwide— serving a population of 320 million. That just shows you how easy it was in the '40s and '50s to obtain a dealership, when the majority of the dealers, like myself years later, inherited no family wealth and had to start from scratch. Ford was virtually awarding dealerships to anybody, regardless of qualifications.

That state of affairs reminded me of something I'd been told in Detroit during my job interview with Ford's vice president, E.D. Longnecker. "A lot of people have been promised they'll one day be head of Ford," he remarked. "The chances of that are very remote. However, there is a place for them in our organization. Just work hard and be patient. That's very important in this company."

Hard work and patience—I kept those attributes in mind in doing my new job and helping others to move forward. One thing that hit me was that I was dealing with myriad money issues now, but had never taken any accounting classes. I needed to fill that void in order to do my job effectively, so I enrolled in a correspondence class in accounting at the University of Florida. I was on the road throughout the week driving between dealerships, giving me abundant study time at night. I kept up with the assignments, passed the tests and, over the course of the year, learned accounting—at least to the point of knowing what a financial statement looked like. All the while, I worked my practice sets by longhand, since we didn't have the benefit of portable calculating devices.

After improving my accounting skills, I realized I needed to know more about economics to get a sense of the bigger picture of finances and trends on the horizon. I signed up for a correspondence class in that subject, once again studying and learning on the run. And in 1958, while all this was going on,

Carol and I welcomed our next child into the world, another beautiful baby girl—Suzanne, whom we called Suzy. Life was now bustling on the home front, while my deeper grasp of business principles was paying off at work. Ford had a school called the Ford Motor Institute and I was fortunate to be selected to attend the program, which offered a week of classes on various topics. My continuing education gave me new tools to help dealers with whatever dilemmas confronted them.

Many dealers had poor inventory systems with no logistics or business plan in place. These were areas I found I could help them with, analyzing their financial operations and determining how they could operate more efficiently. This process served me well in my future business dealings, refining my ability to look at a particular problem and see beyond it toward a potential solution. I approached these situations with a feeling of confidence, and Carol tells me I always took them on with an optimistic, glass-half-full outlook and never shied away from tackling a challenge.

I believed I could forge a better course of action after studying the issues that a particular dealer was encountering, and that we could get the job done if we all worked together. Facing and conquering my own challenges along my path in life—from running the farm as a youth, to learning to fix planes in combat, to immersing myself in learning and teaching after leaving the military—had sharpened my vision for this new stage of my career. My belief that any logistical hurdle could be examined and ultimately surmounted became imbedded in my mindset. And through the years to come—even to this day—I've always been eager to look at new ways of fixing problems or asking how we can do something better.

It helped that I was, and still am, a voracious reader. Books, magazine articles, newspapers all held the ignition key to moving forward effectively, helping me anticipate change and weigh whether one course of action was better than another.

Change is the only constant in this world, and the more you can prepare for it, the better off you'll be. Here's one example: In 1971, I read that the Mazda Corporation planned to bring its cars to the United States. I wrote the home office in Hiroshima: "If you're going to start a dealership organization in the U.S., I'd like to be part of that," I proposed. I wound up becoming the first Mazda dealer in the state of Florida.

I did the same with Isuzu and Infiniti. Again, I wrote a letter to the leadership of those companies and put myself in a position to capitalize on changes in the existing landscape. And I did it with very little money (a good thing because I *had* very little) since these were still untapped brands in America. More recently, I've focused on exploring ways of utilizing compressed natural gas for transportation to make America less dependent on limited and expensive oil resources. But I'm getting ahead of myself—let's return to 1958 and the road my life was following then.

After serving as a sales representative for a year-and-a-half, I began to look for a new way to apply what I'd learned. I had always wanted to join Ford's international department, and the company's language school in Jersey City, caught my interest. Working in the international arena, expanding my boundaries beyond the United States, had always appealed to me. Just as I had done during my Navy days, I volunteered—and I was accepted. On top of that, I received an immediate raise, without ever leaving our house in Jacksonville.

Unfortunately, that didn't sit well with my boss in Jacksonville. Back then, the man you worked for in a major automobile operation essentially controlled your life. He promptly informed me that he was going to block the move, then called the home office in Detroit and said, "You're not going to take Frank. I have plans for him. And we're not going to let him go."

This was completely unanticipated. I'd known what an unpleasant boss he was, never making life easy for any of the representatives in the Jacksonville area. We were constantly on the road, but he'd always insisted we report to our dealership at 8 a.m. Monday morning so he could check on us. And every Saturday, no matter where we were traveling that week, we were required to report for his 9 a.m. meeting that invariably lasted through lunch, which he didn't pay for either!

But that was minor compared to his decision to undermine a step in my career. I was already enrolled in the language school and the plans were underway to send me to Caracas, Venezuela as a manager. In fairness, my boss was probably no different from a lot of the automobile executives of that era, who enjoyed the power they wielded and the ability to control everyone in their operation. Now, his power brought my plans to a screeching halt.

While all this was unfolding, a large retail automobile chain operator in Fort Lauderdale moved into the picture. The owner had been trying for some time to get me to go to work for his business. Unsure of what to do, I drove down to Tampa to consult with a Lincoln-Mercury dealer whom I trusted.: "I'm stymied by my boss in Jacksonville, but I've got this opportunity now in Fort Lauderdale," I told him. "I like Ford Motor Company but I think I need to make a move."

My friend told me he would hire me if he had a position, but he had no openings and encouraged me to think seriously about the job offer. The time was right. I hadn't wished to leave Ford and very well might have built my entire career with the company. Without a doubt, it had been good to me. But circumstances beyond my control had conspired to make me reevaluate my future with the organization. I drove back across the state, made an appointment with my difficult supervisor and —with butterflies in my stomach—informed him that I was quitting for a new job in Fort Lauderdale.

"You can't leave Ford," he responded angrily.

"Well, I just have."

And that's how I moved into the retail car business. Looking back, he did me a huge favor, because it turned out to be the best career move I ever made.

CHAPTER FIVE

Making A Break

At one time or another, everybody finds themselves at a career crossroads, faced with the hazy uncertainty of whether to keep walking down one path or take a gamble and move in a new direction. Some people make impulsive decisions to escape frustrations on the job. They think the other pasture is greener but fail to realize that it can be just as hard to mow. And I've seen many individuals not make it after they leave a company, or wind up just as unhappy in a new one, because they haven't given their situation careful thought.

Sometimes it's simply more comfortable to remain in an imperfect work environment because there may be positives to counter-balance the negatives. Or folks might hesitate to make a move because they'd rather deal with the devil they know than the devil they don't. I understand and appreciate all of that.

But I've always been wired to believe there's a new challenge out there, another adventure to undertake to keep life interesting—even if the road might, at times, lead to places you wish it hadn't. Like a frightening episode that would later arise in which striking union workers tried to harm a member of my family, prompting former heavyweight boxing champion Jersey Joe Walcott to help provide protection– and eventually pulling in the FBI. But more on that later.

The fact is, when you map out a course change, you don't know where life will take you. Despite the uncertainty, I've always been driven to expand my horizons and drawn to opportunities that challenged me, physically or intellectually. Perhaps it's rooted in all the moving around I did in my youth, observing how my father never hesitated to hit the road to earn a living, how he was fascinated by the way things worked and was so skilled in fixing them when they didn't. Maybe it was simply an abiding inner confidence that I could handle whatever came my way.

Looking back, it might well have been easier and less complicated to remain with the Ford Corporation. The company had given me many opportunities during the five years I worked there and I'm sure other doors would have opened had I stuck around. There was even a reasonable chance I could have outlasted my headache-inducing boss. When the "suits" change, as they often do in huge corporations such as Ford, you can get a new break after the dust settles. I recall that one of our neighbors, a longtime Sears employee, practically became apoplectic when I informed him I was leaving Ford. He could not fathom how I could leave one of America's great corporations and the security it afforded me.

Yet I had no desire to endure my boss's unpleasant management style any further, waiting to see what might materialize down the line on Ford's international stage. I'll never know what would have happened had I stayed. With his micro-managing and lack of support, the man had inadvertently nudged me to mull a new opening in the automotive business—a jump from corporate to retail. My gears wouldn't stop spinning over the possibilities.

In 1962, I followed my instincts and joined a Lincoln-Mercury dealership—selling marque cars made, coincidentally, by Ford—in the bustling beach-front city of Fort Lauderdale. From the start, the job provided me with an important experience in managing people. I had a taste of managing in the Navy, but organizing and leading a service department was a new challenge. I embraced my responsibilities to the hilt and, working with a dedicated and talented team, our Lincoln-Mercury service department became No. 1 in the United States. After carefully studying the operation, seeing what worked and what didn't, I determined that the dealership's "traffic flow" needed to be more efficient. And I found a way to fix it—creating a good flow for the automobiles, a good flow for the customers and staff, and a good flow for paperwork. Those things don't just happen on their own: They require a lot of thought, planning and hard work to make everything come together.

My three years at Fort Lauderdale Lincoln-Mercury provided a wonderful education in the inner workings of a successful dealership. I found that I truly enjoyed the daily challenges involved in helping a large operation run well, keeping customers satisfied with excellent service and turning a profit by doing top-notch work. Another key change was in the way we attracted new business. One of my valued employees, Joe Chiavaroli, and I decided to grow the business by acquiring accounts around the state.

We reached out to the local utility company, for instance, and wound up repairing their trucks. We convinced them that they could save money by having us service their vehicles—instead of continuing to pay their own mechanics. Next, we contacted the Florida Highway Patrol. Even though state troopers drove Fords, we encouraged the agency to take its cars to Lincoln-Mercury for repairs. We continued to knock on doors, gaining a foothold in the local Sheriff's Department and telling anyone who'd listen that we wanted their business. We assured them that we'd do it better than anybody else and get their vehicles back on the road quickly—eliminating down time.

I had no desire to leave Fort Lauderdale. Life was good. I'd found a pleasant rental home in a nice neighborhood and painted it before Carol and the girls arrived. That's how

I always liked to do it over the years—take about two or three months in a new job to work 24/7 and learn every conceivable aspect of it, determining what needed to be done to improve the operation. During that transitional period, I'd find a home for us, always re-paint it myself and then bring the family to town when I felt I knew the new business inside and out. That became something of a family tradition—and Carol never misses a chance to remind me that she moved into the first five houses of our marriage without having seen any of them ahead of time.

She and the girls, who both were in now in elementary school, enjoyed the warmth of Fort Lauderdale, in spite of the traffic and occasional swarm of tourists and spring breakers. Carol kept everything running like clockwork at home, doing all sorts of creative things with the girls. I remember one Halloween when she dressed them up as a pair of dice, painting cardboard boxes white with black polka dots.

I enjoyed going to work each morning and was earning better money than I'd made at Ford Motor Company. I also instituted a new program in 1962 to improve customer relations, making it a practice to send a personalized "thank you" note to every customer who had brought his or her vehicle in to be serviced. I took home a stack of repair orders at the end of each day, having created a five-copy carbon repair order system. (Mundane as it sounds, my belief was why do something more than once if you don't have to?)

Just as Carol had been my expert typist in college, she came to my aid once again by typing up thank you notes on 3-by-5 cards that I'd personally sign. Another change we instituted: a list of five questions to ask each person who'd had their car repaired. I hired an outside person to handle this, ensuring that the responses were taken seriously and acted upon if necessary: 1) Were you greeted promptly and courteously? 2) Was your car ready on time? 3) Was your car returned clean? 4) Were the charges explained? 5) Do you have any complaints?

We asked those five questions every day and that approach became a foundation of customer service everywhere I went from then on. Word of the success we enjoyed eventually got around. And in 1965, a new opportunity materialized—in a place I'd given absolutely no thought to moving: Cherry Hill, New Jersey. Not many people would choose to move from Fort Lauderdale to New Jersey. But the owners of our dealership—S.C. Holman and Joe Holman—were headquartered in New Jersey and wanted me to transfer there to implement changes to their Ford dealership, which had been in business since 1922. A meeting was arranged to discuss the topic with my boss and general manager, Frank Hardy—who had become a great mentor to me—and the Holmans, two of the finest people I was ever privileged to work for (and whose family continues to own a number of dealerships today).

I had immense respect for Mr. Hardy. He put a great deal of trust in his managers, gave us the freedom to do our jobs the way we saw fit and didn't impose a heavily structured work environment—a style that would shape my own philosophy throughout my career. I don't believe my general manager had a desire to lose me, but he knew it would be a good career move and, unlike my previous boss, didn't want to stand in the way.

So when the Holmans asked him if I would consider making the move, he didn't hesitate with his response.

"Frank will go to Anchorage, Alaska if it's good for the company—I'm sure he'd be happy to go."

I was called into the office, unaware of the agenda, and they extended their offer—with money that sounded right. I was momentarily caught off guard, but that notion of a new challenge, a new adventure, quickly took hold. At only 34 years old, I was just hitting my stride in the automotive world.

"When do you want me up there? Monday?"

They thought I was kidding. After all, I hadn't even asked to call Carol. But I was dead serious. I sensed a chance to put my experience and acquired skills to use on a bigger stage, with bigger potential rewards. And my father's guiding philosophy was embedded in my genes: Go where the work is. This wasn't building a pipeline but it might be a pipeline to a new career opportunity. Carol was all for the move, even though it meant leaving behind sunny Florida, pulling Leann and Suzy out of school and relocating to a completely unfamiliar part of the world. But by now, she certainly understood what made me tick—a desire to find the next arena to step into, and the self-confidence that I could figure out a way to make things work.

Within a week, I flew north ahead of the family and picked out a new place for us to live in the bustling suburban township of Cherry Hill, eight miles southwest of Philadelphia and truly as much a part of the City of Brotherly Love as its geographical home in southern Jersey. Separated from Philadelphia by the Delaware River and connected to it by the sprawling Benjamin Franklin Bridge, Cherry Hill underwent enormous growth following World War II and was still experiencing a tremendous boom through the Sixties. That meant the prospect of steady growth for my new place of employment and a busy repair schedule for the dealership's incoming service manager.

This particular Ford facility had actually been renovated from an old livery stable—and it looked like that. Right off the bat, I could see there was a lot of room for improvement in the service operation and I got right to work. Based in the hub of the industrial northeast, the dealership sold a lot of big trucks and we wrote 400 repair orders a day. It was a massive amount of work and I realized we needed to create a new way of handling the load efficiently. We transformed the system by creating two shifts instead of one, working from 7 a.m. to 5 p.m. on the first, followed by one lasting from 5 p.m. to 1:30 a.m. We worked long, hard hours to keep up with the non-stop repair demands.

Our new house was only a mile away and I could walk to work each morning. I'd walk home every night for dinner with Carol, Leann and Suzy, and after the girls went to bed around 9 p.m., I'd walk back to the dealership and stay until 1:30. I enjoyed the exercise—it came naturally from a childhood on the farm, walking a mile-plus to the bus stop and always being immersed in physical labor. Every once in a while, manufacturers had issues with their vehicles, which was good and bad. I always told my mechanics that when a factory has problems, that's good for you because you're going to stay employed. As it happened, the frames of many Ford trucks at this time were defective and prone to breaking. That meant we spent a lot of time in Cherry Hill replacing these frames. It was a formidable job, costing several thousand dollars for each one in 1966 when the labor rate was 10 dollars an hour—compared to 100 or more today.

When I arrived, the dealership had been sending many of these vehicles—dump trucks and transport trucks—out to get repaired. That made no sense at all to me. I said, "We're not going to do that—that's a lot of money we're giving away to somebody else." I explained how I planned to change the system. We would handle all the repairs in-house, with our own assembly line working on truck repairs. That was a big innovation—no other dealerships in all of New Jersey or Pennsylvania were taking on the job of handling such tasks. Little by little, our service department in Cherry Hill became Ford's No. 1 operation in the United States.

The biggest issue to overcome—being in the northeast—was the weather. Once winter arrived, we had to contend with snow, and that drove me crazy. What can you do with snow on a 14-acre car lot—especially when you're selling 3,600 new cars and 3,000 used cars a year? You simply did your best to push it out of the way and carry on with business.

One of the other problems we faced was a shortage of skilled mechanics, not just in my shop but in the region. When I arrived, we had 18 on staff but we needed more to help us keep up with the increased workload. The solution: We created our own school, essentially on-the-job training. I hired a man who was a teacher in the Cherry Hill school system to come on site and begin teaching people from the community how to become mechanics. Other Ford dealerships in the area participated in my plan as well, and we served as home base for the apprenticeship training program. We'd send vans to the inner city and bring in men who expressed interest in learning a new trade.

But our operation was different than any other training program. For example, the first step we took was to give trainees their own mechanic uniforms. That gave them a tangible connection to the job, allowing them to go home at night and feel as if they were actually becoming mechanics. Next, we made sure that each apprentice could go out in the field for two hours a day and work with one of our dealership mechanics, whether it was simply changing tires or washing cars. The main thing was that they were around cars and in the presence of trained technicians, working on cars in one way or another from Day One. Our dealership received support for the program from the national On the Job Training program—OJT as it was known—which reimbursed us for half of the costs of the 26-week endeavor.

The program was a huge success in the South Jersey area. We put a lot of men to work, growing my staff of mechanics from 18 to 36 in only a year-and-a-half. That growth was rooted in my core management philosophy, as described earlier: passing responsibility to the lowest common denominator. We followed that basic principle by putting more mechanics on the job to diagnose and solve problems on the ground floor of the operation.

In time, I actually spent time helping to organize several other dealerships in our chain and get them up to speed. In one case, I was brought in as a consultant on a proposed new Ford dealership along the Main Line north of Philadelphia. Because most of the dealers had come up through the sales ranks, they didn't have the knowledge needed for building a new facility in a functional way. Assembling things with an emphasis on functionality became one of my signatures. This was how I put my stamp on any operation I ran: analyzing the situation and figuring out how to achieve optimal performance. When that new Ford dealership was proposed on the Main Line, the builders went to my boss and said, "Can we borrow Frank for a few days to look at the plans?" I came in and scoured all their architectural plans and the nearby roads leading to the proposed dealership—even driving the roads myself to get a better sense of accessibility. When I finished taking stock of all the elements, I sat down with the developers and said, "I don't mean to hurt anybody's feelings, but are you really going to build this facility?" They assured me that they were, so I continued.

"I hate to be blunt, but you couldn't build anything worse. It's in the wrong place to draw customers easily—and it's not going to work."

This was the last thing they wanted to hear. I'm sure they were just hoping that I would provide some tweaks in the plans, not take issue with them completely. But I had to be honest or I wouldn't have been doing my job. I took no offense. For the record, they went ahead and built the dealership—and, five years later, tore it down because it was floundering at that location.

Meanwhile, my ongoing education in the automotive business continued in other ways, beyond honing my expertise in the physical logistics of a dealership. When Ford added a

Harvard MBA program for its executives, inviting two general managers and two service managers from around the country, I was fortunate to be one of the two service managers selected for the special program held in New Jersey. In addition, the organizational and technical knowledge I'd acquired through the years helped shape my managerial style and put my imprint on what I believed to be the most efficient way to run a shop. The key, I had found, was to maintain ongoing communication with all my employees and get their input on what they needed to do their jobs effectively.

I'd ask, "What do you need to be successful at what you're doing?" If they said they didn't need anything, that would be the end of the conversation—but I would expect to see results and performance. If they told me they needed something specific to do the job, I did my best to get whatever it was—and again, I expected results. The idea was to take away possible impediments to success, or excuses for not doing a job well.

Once more, the approach was based on passing responsibility down to the lowest common denominator. Case in point: Many service departments at dealerships have a shop foreman, but I've never seen the need for that position. In my experience, the best person to solve a specific problem is the mechanic dealing directly with that situation. A shop foreman might hear a noise with a car and conclude that the problem lies with a wheel bearing on the right-hand side. The car pulls into the bay and the wheel bearing is replaced, but the customer still hears the noise when he drives home. He or she comes back upset and all the mechanic can do is tell the foreman: "Well, you're the one who told me to replace the wheel bearing." In other words, the mechanic was given no chance to have input into the process—something that happens far too many times. That's why I chose not to have foremen in my shops and still don't to this day. I firmly believe it should be the mechanics' role—the person at the ground level of the process—to diagnose and fix a problem.

Now if a mechanic was unable to determine the cause of a problem, that's when I'd tell them to come to me and we'd both take a look to see if we could figure it out together. But if you take that step first, you haven't passed responsibility to the person tasked with assessing and correcting problems on the front line. We've worked hard to incorporate this approach into our management style. Our car washers are the ones who buy chemicals to wash the cars because they know precisely what it takes. That's not my expertise—I only know how to make coffee so why would I tell them what they need to do their job right? My role is to keep asking questions. That's how to learn precisely what your employees need to succeed, and to take direct ownership of their work.

Carol may have described my approach best: "Frank's management style is to teach his people and then let them work on their own. Once he gives them responsibility, he rarely butts back in. He says, 'This is what I expect' and lets them run with it. If they make a mistake, he steps back in or lets them figure out what their mistake was. But he stays pretty hands off. That's why I've gotten to run the house all these years without any interference from him."

There is a fundamentally important offshoot of this approach: by allowing people to be invested in the decision-making process, by letting them do their jobs, it empowers them and makes them feel more fulfilled in their work. Happy employees tend to be more productive employees. And that, in turn, makes for better overall performance and a more successful business.

I've read many books on leadership—and remain a voracious reader of all kinds of books—and that has certainly helped inform my management style. One book, Management by Walking Around, has particularly resonated with me. Long before the book came out in 1982, I found the practice of moving through the work place and engaging with employees to be highly productive and beneficial. I later served as a speaker on a panel with one of the co-authors and enjoyed sharing how that walking-and-talking approach with my employees had worked so well for me through the years.

Cherry Hill was a key step in the growth of my leadership style. The move from Florida to New Jersey hadn't been an easy one at first for Carol and the kids, but they grew accustomed to the brisker pace of life and harsher weather. I have to credit Carol for doing so much for the girls while I worked long, tiring days. She did a truly wonderful job as a mother. It wasn't always easy for our kids to make the adjustment to a new home, and Carol was the one who had to help them get through the tough times. At first, Leann absolutely hated moving to Cherry Hill, but with lots of support and understanding, she gradually got over her anger and made new friends, winding up having the most fun she remembered during her childhood.

In the summer, Leann and Suzy had lemonade stands and played outside until dark. And we always shared as many activities together as possible—eating dinner and telling stories from the day, watching TV shows with a bowl of popcorn, going to neighborhood picnics and attending the girls' school chorus concerts—though I've been reminded that I dozed off a time or two while sitting with Carol in the audience after a long, hard day at work. You could say it was a Leave It To Beaver existence with a touch of Father Knows Best. If there was one virtue I always stressed, it was the importance of being honest, and that there would be consequences for failing to be. I'd learned that basic rule from my parents, and the girls paid attention—probably because I drummed it into their heads on a regular basis throughout their childhood.

Though I had no fondness for snow, the kids both loved playing in it, ice-skating in the streets and sledding down a dead-end street near the house. Every year, a different dad got to dress up as Santa Claus and ride on the fire truck in a Christmas parade in town. And I remember how excited both girls were when it was my turn to be Old St. Nick, waving to the families lining the street.

The success we enjoyed in Fort Lauderdale and Cherry Hill eventually opened the door to a new career move in 1969: my first general manager job, running a Lincoln-Mercury dealership, Merlin Motors, in neighboring Camden. This was a notch higher in prestige and responsibility, as well as pay, and I loved the challenge of running an entire operation. My work overseeing service departments had prepared me well for this new step in my career. But I would soon learn that expanded leadership and responsibility came with a price.

Shortly after I assumed my new role, the local mechanics union went on strike. Prior to the work stoppage, we engaged in a series of negotiations that produced nothing but escalating tensions. We hired one of the nation's leading labor law firms, based in Atlanta, to help guide us through the maze of demands and counteroffers. Finally, the strike was called and the situation quickly got nasty. Our phones at the dealership were tapped, as was my phone at home, and union members went house to house in our neighborhood trying to get information about us. But the scariest moment occurred one day when Suzy went down to the end of the driveway to take out the garbage, with our dog scurrying out the door after her. Out of nowhere, a car careened toward her from across the street and slammed into the trash bin. Suzy was terrified but thankfully unharmed, but our dog, a sweet little Pug named Sam, was struck, injuring its hind legs and leaving it with a permanent limp.

We had police protection from then on. The security detail included help from aforementioned former boxing champ Jersey Joe Walcott, who enjoyed his heyday in the ring during the 1940s and '50s. Now, he was serving as Camden's safety commissioner, overseeing the police and fire department—and leasing 50 cars at the time from our company. He was an impressive man and a real friend. Jersey Joe made sure that patrolmen were around us at all times to protect us from threats and potential violence.

I still feel grateful for that protection. One day, a union organizer came to the dealership unannounced, violating a provision that union representatives could not come on our property during the strike. Jersey Joe promptly ordered a search and seizure of the car. Police opened up the trunk and found it filled with weapons. Whether the man intended to use them we don't know, but, to say the least, it was an unsettling experience.

We did what we could to protect ourselves. On occasion, we resorted to turning on our lawn sprinkler system to disperse picketers and break up the crowd boycotting the dealership. Fortunately, we always had a great relationship with the police department to help us through that trying time. Every morning for weeks, I had to drive from Cherry Hill to Philadelphia and meet at 7 a.m. with FBI agents at their field office, providing whatever information they requested to keep them updated. After seven weeks, the strike was finally settled with five cent pay increases. Business slowly returned to a normal pace, but tension lingered and things never felt quite the same.

As it happened, another potential opportunity was taking shape. A dealership owner I'd gotten to know in Los Angeles wanted me to consider taking over as general manager at one of his stores and get it running up to its potential. Carol and I were familiar enough with California from the war years, and my having worked on developing airplanes and bombing maneuvers for the Navy. There was something about moving onto a bigger dealership stage—figuring out how to make a business as successful as possible—that instantly appealed to me.

A cross-country move wasn't exactly the news that Carol, Leann or Suzy wanted to hear, having admirably settled into a new life in New Jersey. But the tumultuous strike experience probably made it easier for them to be open to a fresh start. A new adventure was at hand, with the path now pointing toward another challenge. Once again, it was time to go west.

CHAPTER SIX

"That's Life"

The big move to Southern California would come with a touch of Hollywood and celebrity sightings—including "Old Blue Eyes" himself, Frank Sinatra, patronizing my new place of work. But we might never have headed to the star-studded corner of the world in the first place had I not agreed to lunch one summer day in 1969 at a ritzy spot in its own right—the legendary Plaza Hotel, perched on the pristine edge of Central Park in Manhattan. I had driven up from Cherry Hill to meet with a man who owned a thriving Volkswagen dealership in Beverly Hills and a busy Porsche and Lincoln-Mercury store nearby in Inglewood. I sensed that my life was about to change.

I'd seen his sales statements and the numbers were impressive. He told me how much he wanted to bring me out to California and help him run the dealerships, and even promised me a percentage of the businesses. I didn't know him particularly well but it was hard to argue with the success of his operations and flattering to be pursued with such eagerness. "Why don't you quit your job and join me, Frank?" he prodded.

This seemed like a logical step forward in the progression of my career. And in a matter of weeks, Carol and I were loading up our station wagon for the 3,000-mile trek across the country. In the same year that Neil Armstrong would set foot on the moon, we were taking our own giant leap into a future that appeared full of new possibilities. Leann and Suzy were real troupers, riding in the back seat with our dog, Sam, who unfortunately decided it was a good idea to bark at passing cars most of the trip. As I recall, we broke down somewhere in Indiana in the midst of a hot spell, and perhaps that was a sign of things to come.

It didn't take long after arriving and starting my new job to notice various irregularities in the accounting records. Then, about two weeks later, came the real eye-opener: my boss slurring his words and stumbling into my office, barely able to walk from being intoxicated. If you've ever worked for a boss with a daily drinking problem, I assure you it's not a great experience. As difficult as Cherry Hill had become, I absolutely could not believe what I'd suddenly gotten myself into. I'd uprooted my family and left behind a flawed yet still secure work situation in New Jersey for a potential nightmare. "I've sunk my ship," I thought to myself. Everything about the dealership was bad. The books were dishonest and I knew I couldn't live in that environment very long.

One of the first things I noticed was the owner's preoccupation with antique vehicles—he had about 100 of them, gorgeous old cars that he had painstakingly restored. He employed a man fulltime to work on the array of vintage Model-T's, Duesenbergs, Packards and other famous brands, and seemed as interested in this pursuit as in selling our new cars. It quickly became clear to me that he was siphoning off money from the business to support this expensive habit. But it wasn't as if I could easily quit on the spot, having dragged Carol and the kids from their comfortable life in Jersey smack into my troubles in paradise.

We'd already moved into a beautiful home on a mountainside overlooking Will Rogers State Park and the posh suburb of Brentwood, some 25 years before it would become world famous as the home of O.J. Simpson amid his infamous murder trial. Carol would go down to the grocery store in town and see all kinds of familiar faces on any given day, like Harry Morgan, who played Colonel Potter on M*A*S*H. They were just regular folks doing their shopping. And our new home was certainly a far cry from our previous houses. Looking out the window over the beautiful mountain, Carol and I would discuss the latest round of headaches I'd dealt with earlier in the day. I had no other job to jump to and simply had to make the best of a bad situation while being alert to any new opportunities that might arise.

In spite of my frustrations, the overall experience had its share of elements that Carol aptly described as "interesting." For example, one of the Beverly Hills employees, a Volkswagen salesman, was married to a movie writer for a Greek newspaper. She attended many of the marquee actor previews and we were occasionally invited along. One night, we wound up at a party in the home of TV star Leonard Nimoy, whose character, Mr. Spock, had become a household name from the hit show, Star Trek. We were certainly aware of the program's popularity, though Leann and Suzy were far more attuned to the significance of Spock, Captain Kirk and the Starship Enterprise. And they were considerably more excited than we were about our visit to the actor's house. He wore his pointy Vulcan ears at the party the whole time—and struck both Carol and me as really weird, regardless of his pop-culture notoriety.

There was no shortage of unusual people in our path, it seemed. The parts manager for the VW dealership was a member of the iconic European banking family, the Rothschilds, and every quarter he had to take off five days to attend board meetings in Paris. Of all our customers, the one who caught everybody's attention was Sinatra. We'd receive word when he planned to come, and let him in late at night after closing, allowing him to shop without causing a stir. On one such excursion he purchased three Ferrari Lussos—one for daughter Nancy, one for Frank Jr. and one for himself. Another connection to the famous singer occurred when we hired a young woman to help look after Leann and Suzy after they got home from junior high school. It turned out she worked for Sinatra. She'd take them to places like Hollywood and Vine and they'd go stargazing; one time they ran into comedian Flip Wilson and got his autograph. From their perspective, the move to Los Angeles had its distinct benefits, though neither of the girls cared for the daily layer of smog that hovered over Brentwood.

For me, the sequence of events from Cherry Hill to LA felt more like lyrics from my fellow Frank's hit, *That's Life*: "riding high in April, shot down in May." But there was also the line about getting "back on top in June," and a new door was about to open that would change everything.

Carol and I knew we had to find a way out of the mess. I'd tried to buy a Chevrolet dealership in San Bernardino, but that had fallen through. Then we looked north of Los Angeles, just beyond the San Fernando Valley, in Santa Barbara. Our new exit strategy was to attempt to purchase a Buick dealership there. We thought there was a good chance the deal would get done and even went house shopping, picking out a wonderful Spanish place with an indoor patio. But before we finalized anything, I received a long-distance call from a woman named Marylou Herndon. She was the wife of Homer Herndon in Tampa, where her husband owned a Mercedes, Toyota and Volvo dealership. I'd known Homer for many years—dating back to my time in Jacksonville—and Marylou explained that his health was in decline. At age 65, he was seeking somebody to help him run his operation. My name was at the top of his list.

"Homer's not doing well. Are you happy where you are?" she asked.

The answer, obviously, was a resounding no. There was still an unknown factor involved with the Santa Barbara Buick dealership. The deal wasn't final, for one thing, and it was more of a stop-gap move to get away from a bad situation. The idea of returning to Florida, where we had roots and many good memories in Jacksonville and Fort Lauderdale, was instantly appealing. Carol and I arranged a visit back to Tampa to meet with the Herndons and the deal came together, with Homer giving me 15-percent of the business. Soon after, on August 20, 1970, I arrived in Tampa to make a new start.

Neither of us could have any hint of how, as we developed a deepening bond with the area in the years to come, this move would ultimately alter our lives. Once again, I was going where the work was. "And once again," Carol likes to remind me with her trademark dry wit, "I got left behind." She stayed back with the girls while I got settled into the new surroundings. Unfortunately, their surroundings became quite harrowing after I left—wildfires began to sweep through the California mountainside. Thank goodness, the fires stayed far enough away for Carol and the girls to remain safe, and they joined me in Tampa just in time for Thanksgiving.

By then, I was well-entrenched in my new job. Homer was a sweet man, but working with him wasn't always easy. He was very old school in his approach to business. He didn't want to relinquish control, hesitated to pay for accounting or legal advice and kept his accounts on small pieces of paper in his pockets. But he did give me enough room to help him deal with some issues, bringing about an improvement of sales through proper management.

One area I could not help him with was his passion for greyhounds. Homer had more than 500 dogs, racing them in Florida and as far away as Boston and Seattle, and raising them in Florida, Arkansas, Oklahoma and the Midwest. The problem was that the money to support this endeavor came from the dealerships. And here's the thing about dogs: they eat every day. The cost for feeding that many was astronomical. In the early 1960s, Homer had one world champion, a greyhound named Rinaker, and probably made some money with him. But I never detected any other possible profit from his greyhound business while I was there. I wasn't the least bit interested in greyhound racing—I just had to pay the formidable bills that kept piling up.

All the while, Homer's health continued to fail and he passed away a year after I joined him, in August 1971. Marylou, his widow, had no desire to keep the business, since they had no children to take it over. I knew this was an opportunity to finally run my own dealership. So I borrowed $5,000 from my brother, $10,000 from a friend named Herb Overstreet and $240,000 from First Florida Bank. It was a stressful experience, having to ask for so much money—in fact, I wound up with a case of hives. But in the end, I had enough cash to buy out Marylou Herndon's share and officially take charge of my first dealership.

One of my first moves was to liquidate the greyhound business and focus entirely on selling and servicing automobiles. In April of 1970—five months before my arrival—Homer had just finished building a new dealership for his Mercedes and Volvo dealerships at the corner of Buffalo (which later became Martin Luther King Jr. Blvd.) and Florida Avenue. We also had a Toyota dealership nearby, an old building I nicknamed "The Fruit Stand" because it was so rickety in appearance. Homer didn't want to spend any money on that, because imports were still viewed with skepticism. When I bought the business, I had a special plan for that Toyota operation.

As a point of historic reference, we were the only Toyota dealer in Hillsborough County. I felt strongly that we needed to have new facilities, so I purchased land on Florida Avenue and 109th and we built a new home for the dealership, with a grand opening for University Toyota in February 1973. Nobody else wanted anything to do with Toyota at the time—can you imagine that? I had a friend who told me, "That car's not going to sell. It's a piece of junk. We don't need to worry about imports."

I'm not claiming that I had a special hunch about Toyota's viability. As I mentioned earlier in these pages, when you don't have a lot of money, you do whatever you have to do. The automobile industry has always been very expensive to enter, and I'd already borrowed extensively to buy out Mrs. Herndon's share of the business. Carol had even gone back to work at a resort on the east side of the Courtney Campbell Causeway to help with our home finances. My best option for a new dealership was with a more affordable company, Toyota, which badly wanted to make inroads in the United States. Simply put, the Japanese automaker gave me a way to get into the game on a larger scale.

Before I went to the bank, I reached out to longtime Chevrolet dealer Jim Ferman, Sr., to see if he wanted to join me as an investor, and he remarked, "I don't want anything to do with those imports." But years later, he told me, "I made a mistake on that one!"

Without an investor, my only option was to go back to the bank. Fortunately, at that time, they were much easier to deal with than they are today. There's no way you could get into business now the way I did then. The bank's chairman of the board, George Holsinger, also happened to be the Ford dealer in town and I had occasionally called on him when I worked for the Lincoln-Mercury division in Florida. The connection helped when it came time to make my pitch to the loan committee at the old First Florida Bank building in downtown Tampa. The people in charge of approving or denying the loan had all kinds of questions for me, and I wasn't sure if they were sold. Finally, George interjected, "Look, this boy's going to pay us back. Give him the damn money!" And that was the end of the conversation.

As the only Toyota dealer in town, we did reasonably well, averaging about 50 sales a month. That doesn't sound like much, but keep in mind that the import business was still in its infancy in America, and consumers really didn't know the Toyota brand. It still had a questionable reputation, as many Japanese products did at that time. The truth is, my Mercedes dealership didn't sell a tremendous number of the luxury cars, either—only 75 a year—when I took over. But believe it or not, that was still enough to rank my store as one of the biggest of its kind in Florida. Mercedes as a company sold just 8,000 cars in the United States when I became a dealer in 1971. Today that number tops 300,000 nationwide. That just shows you how vastly different the import landscape was in the early '70s. If you weren't there in the middle of it, you wouldn't fully appreciate how far things have come in today's import-heavy world.

Life in Tampa was comfortable from the start. We settled into a new neighborhood and pleasant house in Carrollwood. Carol says she made sure we bought the house in Tampa right away because she was finished moving, though we still owned the mountainside house in California. When we arrived, Leann was in the ninth grade and Suzy the seventh, and soon each was attending Chamberlain High School. It was impressive to see how well they both handled the frequent moves and disruptions in their lives.

Leann started working at several of the dealerships in high school and, when she turned 16, I surprised her with her first car—a 1969 baby blue Toyota Corona. Her recollection of that moment makes me smile: "Dad took us to the Mercedes dealership and wanted us to go into the shop. Suzy and I were thinking, 'Okay, why do we need to come here, this is boring. Then dad said, 'Hey, why is that Toyota in the Mercedes shop?' I had no clue and really did not care. But he went, 'That's your car.'

And all of a sudden, I cared! That was the sweetest car, I loved it—and I loved the way my dad thought of surprising me."

I gave Suzy a used yellow Corolla for her Sweet 16th, and she was just as thrilled as her sister had been. She told me that her friends at school wondered why I hadn't given her a brand new Mercedes, but that's not the lesson I wanted to impart. I wanted my girls to appreciate what they had, work hard, always be honest, remain humble and be kind to people. Suzy worked at the dealerships just like her sister. They weren't given a pass simply because I was their father—they had to pull their own weight with whatever tasks they had, even if it was counting nuts and bolts for hours on end or filing stacks of old service orders. As Suzy recalls, "I don't know if they knew I'd be working there over the summer and he saved all those jobs up for me, but it was certainly tedious and unglamorous!"

Carol and I made a point of traveling with the girls. Every summer from the time they were young children, we'd take them on vacations—often driving across the United States to visit relatives or just see the country. In our industry, they have what is called "20 Groups," composed of 20 dealers from various geographic areas of the state, who would get together three times a year—maybe one time in Vancouver, British Columbia, or Montreal or Jackson Hole, Wyoming. These were three-day meetings in which we would exchange financial statements and evaluate each other's businesses. We'd stretch them to five or six days and make a vacation out of it, often taking the girls with us during the school year, when classes were in session, and naturally that made it even more fun for them. Wherever we went, I always felt travel was a wonderful part of their education and opened their eyes to the world.

There was much to see and appreciate on the home front in the 1970s as well. Tampa and the surrounding area was in the midst of a growth spurt. In 1971, Tampa International Airport had come into existence—the same year that Disney World opened its doors 90 minutes away near Orlando, bringing new waves of tourism to the region.

By 1975, the Tampa Bay Rowdies had brought their high-energy, well-marketed North American Soccer League team to the area, attracting a devoted following as the sport began to take hold in America. And the National Football League was about to launch a new franchise with the birth of the Tampa Bay Buccaneers in 1976. Even with their much-publicized 0-26 start as a franchise, the Bucs and the NFL had helped put the Tampa Bay area on the map in a way that it had never previously enjoyed.

As for the area colleges, there wasn't much to talk about. The University of Tampa downtown was not yet considered the fine institution it would eventually become. And the school that Homer and Marylou Herndon had driven us by when we visited—the University of South Florida—basically consisted of two buildings, the library and the administration office. USF had opened in 1956 and still wasn't much to look at on the sparse stretch along Fowler Avenue—some 1,700 acres of nondescript land that had been home to a Henderson Air Field bombing range during World War II. We could never have imagined the role this modest location would one day play in our lives.

Beyond Tampa Bay, Florida as a whole was beginning its own slow growth surge. When we first moved to Jacksonville, the population stood at four million. By the time we came back to live in 1971, the number had grown to some seven million—on its way to thirteen million in 1990 and twenty million, the third most populous state in the country today. Florida in general and Tampa in particular began to feel like home. It was an exciting time to be building my own business amid all this change. As part of the natural progression, we started to get involved in the community—something we'd never had time for in the past.

I'd always thought that the Chamber of Commerce had a vital role in a town, so after buying the dealerships I introduced myself to the Tampa Chamber of Commerce president, Scott Christopher, explaining that I'd like to join and serve in whatever capacity was needed. That was the beginning of a long relationship with the Chamber. At the same time, I signed up with the North Tampa Rotary Club, and Carol and I joined the Methodist Church in Carrollwood and then the downtown Tampa Methodist Church. Our mutual feelings about the importance of higher education motivated me to reach out to the University of Tampa, and I became a member of the Board of Counselors from 1974-76 (and later the Board of Trustees, where I became Vice Chairman).

Meanwhile, the automobile business was good. In 1976, I opened an all-new Precision Motorcar dealership on North Dale Mabry Highway to sell Mercedes. I purchased a Ford store in Brooksville, Fla., naming it Freedom Ford in honor of the nation's Bicentennial, and would soon be opening a Nissan dealership in Lexington, Ky. In addition, when I assumed control of the Toyota store, I took charge of several other import dealerships Homer had acquired, such as Fiat, British Leland, German Ford and Taunus. As a side note, Fiat is the only car I ever sold that "disintegrated" on the show room floor; the door literally fell off, not the ideal way to attract customers. But most of our dealings went well, especially as Toyota became increasingly familiar to consumers and we established a track record for success.

After so many moves to different parts of the country, we were glad to feel settled, to be putting down roots. And at a certain point, we decided we should start investing in our community.

We started on a small scale, like donating money to support Chamberlain High's newspaper when the girls worked on it. We were generous in tithing with our church, as we had been in Cherry Hill. In fact, we gave a car to our minister and another to the Tampa Chamber of Commerce. We also started a tradition of giving a Mercedes to Bucs' head coaches, beginning with John McKay and continuing through Tony Dungy's tenure. (We respected Coach Dungy a great deal and ended our involvement with the Bucs after he was let go in 2000). Our first truly significant gift came with the creation of the H. Lee Moffitt Cancer Center in Tampa—a gift spurred by the cancer death of one of my men. Plans were announced for the center in 1978, groundbreaking began in 1983, and the cutting-edge facility opened in 1986.

But I was also getting involved on another track, with a new pursuit I viewed as deeply important: having a hand in the creation of public policy. It all began with the Nixon Administration's questionable effort to combat inflation by implementing wage and price controls—a policy that was proving devastating to automobile dealers. Here's an example of how the program hurt us: Let's say one customer has decided to trade in an eight-year-old car with 150,000 miles, a car worth only $8,000. Another person trades in the same model, but one with only 30,000 miles, and this one is worth $20,000. With wage and price controls, I would be required to allow the same amount on both trades, despite the fact that the first car has far more wear and tear.

The policy was completely unbalanced and unfair and instantly put a vise on our business. In an attempt to change this, we held a meeting at the Shoreham Hotel in Washington, D.C. to find a way to rid the business community of wage and price controls. This marked the start of my involvement in public policy. I joined the board of the International Automobile Dealers Association to fight the measures—and our efforts made a difference. By January 1973, wage and price controls were made less restrictive and later removed altogether.

But the biggest turning point came one day in early 1976, completely by accident—at a seemingly mundane moment. To give you some background, I have always firmly believed that the boss should open and read all incoming mail at a dealership, and I've instructed my general managers to follow that practice. From reading the incoming mail, I've discovered a great deal about my business—including ways that people can steal or be influenced by outsiders, by banks and businesses offering special treatment for something in return. If you are ignorant about these possible enticements, I guarantee that your company will run into trouble. And here's another reason for reading the incoming mail: The practice can also lead to opportunity.

To get back to that moment in 1976, none of the mail I was opening seemed out of the ordinary—until I opened an envelope addressed to the dealership containing a letter to a person whose name I didn't recognize.

The letter explained that a Small Business Council was being created within the United States Chamber of Commerce, and asked if he would be interested in joining. I could hardly believe such a phenomenal opportunity had arrived completely inadvertently. It was one of the best mistakes that ever came down the pike. I immediately wrote a letter stating that I wasn't the intended recipient, but explained who I was and that I would very much like to be considered. In short order, I received a response inviting me to join the Small Business Council.

That serendipitous correspondence was the beginning of what would be my extensive involvement in public policy—and more fun over the next 20 years than I could ever have imagined.

CHAPTER SEVEN

Lessons to Live (and Manage) By

I can say this without reservation: The amazing adventure that lay before me at this moment, the myriad experiences that would soon define the direction of my career and enrich my life, could never have happened had it not been for certain key business lessons I'd learned and adopted by this point as part of my management style. Without those, I would not have been able to travel around the world with Carol, become Chairman of the Board of the U.S. Chamber of Commerce, or work with Presidents Carter, Reagan and Bush, or enjoy so many other high points of my career described in the chapters to follow.

But before going further in my story, I'd like to pause and examine some key insights I had gained by this time in my life—insights culled from on-the-job situations that would become forged into core beliefs and guiding tenets. Think of this chapter not as an intermission, but as a chance to reflect, review and set the stage for the second act. In short, everything that followed was made possible by what came before, and all the vital lessons learned along the way.

First, it's worthwhile to revisit the chief lesson I learned in the Navy, one that formed the essence of my approach to managing people.

Manage to the Lowest Common Denominator: As I described earlier, I observed how the entire Navy system was built on giving each person in the chain responsibility for performing a specific duty, for handling an assigned task. I saw firsthand that the success of an operation hinged on the delegation from top to bottom of certain responsibilities, and I learned how deeply the system depended on individuals—wherever they ranked in that chain of command—performing their jobs to the best of their ability. In the Navy, it could mean the difference between life and death. In business the same principle can mean the difference between success and failure.

When I ran service departments and then dealerships, I not only expected my employees to do their specific jobs, I trusted them to do those jobs without being micromanaged by a hovering superior. As I stated earlier, I expect the person in charge of cleaning the cars to know what supplies are needed for the job, and to take responsibility for purchasing them so that the work can be done in an exemplary fashion. It's not my job to know those details, and it is not the job of the GM or service manager. Our responsibility is to manage to the lowest common denominator—to define the job, select qualified employees and to let them do the job expected of them. This accomplishes a simple but highly significant result. By giving people the freedom to take charge and ownership of the work they have been assigned, you're showing them respect. And, in return, they will respect you.

The importance of this system in a successful, thriving business can't be overstated. And it lies at the heart of what evolved into my overriding method of operating a company.

Decentralized Management vs. Centralization: I have created a decentralized company structure from the start. General Motors is an example of a failed centralized company, in which all the decisions are made by a very small group of people who don't involve people below them in the process. I've always preferred to have my managers put their personal stamp on the business they're running. I used to tell them jokingly, "I'm lazy, so you have to work like hell to support me." The point is that I gave them the reins to run their own branch of the company, and that is the type of management style I've chosen because I've seen the results.

I played golf with a car dealer recently who was on his smart phone the entire time we were on the course, talking to his managers constantly to tell them this or that. If you micromanage to that extent, and many people do so at companies large and small, employees don't get a chance to spread their wings. They can grow frustrated, and generally fail to do their best work. The good performers will invariably leave for a place that gives them a chance to achieve their potential.

By contrast, I always placed a great deal of trust in people to do their jobs well—rewarding them accordingly—and they trusted me in return. My belief is that everybody wants to excel, so I give him or her the opportunity. That doesn't mean I haven't had to replace anyone along the way. But on balance, I've had to replace very few. The credit for that goes partly to my method for hiring new employees. I really try to learn about backgrounds—how people were raised, whether they've demonstrated a strong work ethic, and what their value system is. To me, those factors are more important than a resume. In fact, I've been known to take an applicant's resume during an interview and act like I'm throwing it away. I'll say, "I'm just going to place this in my round file and then we'll talk." I try to make people comfortable, because everyone is nervous when they come in for an interview. A little bit of humor helps put people at ease in that situation and breaks the ice, often paving the way for a more meaningful give and take with a person you may decide to invest in.

The Four Pillars of Managing: I wrote in a previous chapter about Frank Hardy, my general manager at the Lincoln-Mercury

Dealership in Fort Lauderdale. Frank is a terrific example of the impact a good leader and manager can have on his staff. One of the reasons we enjoyed so much success at the dealership was the tone Frank set, making it possible for everyone to do his or her best work. He was the embodiment of what I came to adopt as the essence of my management philosophy—the belief that everybody works for four essential things:

- Respect

- Satisfaction

- Recognition

- Compensation

The points are largely self-explanatory. If you show respect for the people who work for you, they will respect you. Furthermore, my view is that everybody works for satisfaction, recognition and compensation, in that order. That's how you motivate people. Employees need to get satisfaction out of their job, and they want to be recognized for doing it well. A pat on the back or words of praise can make a world of difference, in the same way being paid fairly makes an employee feel valued.

I once told a reporter, "There are two types of management styles today—the fear system and the reward system. We try to operate on the reward system." When employees are happy and feel appreciated, they are going to do their best work—and that benefits everybody. That's why I always made a practice of giving my general managers a minority ownership of the business, created a profit sharing system and maintained a policy against laying off employees in lean times.

My goal was and has always been to engender trust and loyalty, and I'm gratified to know that I have a good number of employees who have been with my company for 30 and 40 years. One of them, P.J. Thomas, began in my Toyota store in

1977 and now works as office manager at our Mazda store. Her sentiments bring a smile to my face.

"Over the past 30 years, I've worked at two other places for a very short time. That's how I learned what a different kind of a businessperson Frank is, what a different kind of a boss he is. He is the most honest person I've ever met in my life. And he's the most decent and generous man when it comes to treating his employees well. He has one philosophy: treat your people right—the way you'd want to be treated.

I can't even tell you the number of people who once worked for Frank and call here, wanting to work for him again. We all know we've been treated right and fairly. He's a strict business-man and you have to know how he wants things done. But you know that it's the right thing to do: We treat customers right, we treat our employees right and we work hard. If you do those things, you never, ever fear that you won't have a job."

The rewards of treating people the right way were always obvious as far as I was concerned. The bosses I had who were good to me made me want to work even harder, and those who showed little or no appreciation made me want to look else-where for a job. That's why I have never had a question about the most effective way of managing people.

I sincerely hope that these few principles, so important to my own life, can be building blocks for others as they forge their own futures. Tested and honed by experience, those principles guided me through the years ahead in the pages that follow.

CHAPTER EIGHT

A Big Voice for Small Business

As a registered Republican, I never imagined how my life would change after Democratic candidate Jimmy Carter took the oath of office in January 1977 to become our country's 39th president. Getting involved with the Carter Administration was the last thing on my mind, but the best thing that could have happened at that time. Carter's interest in small business, stemming from his background as a Georgia peanut farmer, set in motion the chain of events that led me to Washington and into the world of public policy—thanks to that letter I received from out of the blue.

In this new phase of my professional life, I did everything I could to create a more favorable national climate for the growth of small businesses. As part of the U.S. Chamber of Commerce, I flew across the country to promote our agenda, testified before Congress and sometimes gave multiple talks in different parts of the country in a single day. It was the ride of a lifetime that would take Carol and me around the world through three U.S. presidential administrations, numerous speeches in Europe and Asia in the presence of foreign leaders—and even a seat at a celebrity-driven White House dinner party beside a Hollywood superstar and the Secretary of State.

The Small Business Council was established soon after Carter took office and I was excited to become involved in it as a director of the U.S. Chamber of Commerce. The Chamber consisted of mostly Fortune 500 companies back then and creating a small business outreach was a significant development. Small business was growing. My own burgeoning business—Automotive Management Services, Inc.—was an example. Combined sales six years earlier, when I acquired my first two dealerships in 1971, totaled less than $4 million, with a work force of 35. But as 1980 approached, I'd increased my number of employees to 175 and added dealerships in Lakeland, Lexington, Ky. and Albany, Ga. with various brands of cars—Oldsmobile, Chrysler-Dodge, BMW and Mercedes-Benz. Though the automobile market was taking a beating amid rampant inflation and the sagging economy of the late 1970s, our overall sales surpassed $530 million, with 5,600 new and used cars sold.

I was interviewed at the time by Nation's Business magazine and remarked, "My banker wants to know why I'm always buying more dealerships. Well, it is my belief that a growing company is easier to run than one that is stagnant. We will always be expanding and growing. But it is important that you know how to merchandise and sell your product." I also believed it was important to create a positive atmosphere in your business, one that promotes from within and encourages participation in decision-making. That contributes to the overall health of your company and is why I always discussed key corporate decisions with my managers. Transparency was and is our hallmark. By now, though, I was spending about half my time directly overseeing my dealerships and the other half advocating for small businesses.

Some of the latter pursuit was done under the auspices of the International Executive Service Corps, an organization created by the U.S. ambassador to Panama, Sol Linowitz, and banker David Rockefeller. With the support of the IESC, executives such as myself traveled the world helping developing countries in business matters. Carol and I went to Panama for three months in 1977 in this capacity, while negotiations were underway with the U.S. to turn the 60-year-old Panama Canal over to Panama. We learned firsthand why the Panamanians harbored such bitter feelings toward America: during the entire history of the Canal, only one Panamanian had been trained as a pilot there. The rest were from the United States, earning cushy six-figure salaries. In fact, we witnessed rude and dismissive behavior on the part of many Americans during our visit, regrettably reinforcing the "Ugly American" image running rampant there.

When I returned to Washington to speak at a meeting of the U.S. Chamber, I was asked about my impressions of Panama. I said, "Well, most of you in this room will disagree with me, but it's time there was a change." My strong belief was that Panama should be given control of the Canal and invested in its own future. Carol and I were ambivalent about the issue when we first arrived in the country, but after learning how poorly we treated the Panamanians—never bothering even to train them—we changed our minds. We met so many U.S. officials who never bothered to leave the small Canal Zone compound and actually set foot in Panama, or try to understand the plight of the Panamanian people. The American people were certainly misinformed on the situation and I felt a responsibility to shed light on an injustice. This formative experience may well have sparked the philanthropic interests that would one day burn strong for us—reinforcing the notion that helping others is an important part of life.

Meanwhile, there was plenty of work to do on the home front, especially in the nation's capital in my role as Chairman of the Chamber's Council on Small Business. One of the biggest issues of the day was the aforementioned inflation, ballooning in the wake of the 1973 Arab Oil Embargo and the 1979 energy crisis. Inflation had dipped to 5.8 percent at the start of Carter's administration but was flying off the charts at 13.5 percent in

1980. As I told Nation's Business magazine, "Inflation impacts more on small business than on any other sector because of the base which we have to cover our costs. It is inconceivable that there are those in the administration who castigate small business as the cause of inflation. Small business is the victim rather than the perpetrator."

Against that backdrop, in early 1980, President Carter and his staff organized the White House Conference on Small Business. I was officially appointed to it by a fixture of Florida's political scene, longtime U.S. Representative Sam Gibbons of Tampa. On January 13, 1980, the President welcomed us heartily, acknowledging the challenges facing America—from economic woes to the hostage crisis with Iran—while emphasizing the importance of small business to the nation's well-being. "Just as we must keep bright the beacon of human freedom, demonstrate national unity, and maintain the military strength of our country, so must we also maintain a national economy that will make all this possible," he told our gathering. "To me, that means a further strengthening of the small businesses of America. I know firsthand this must be. I'm one of the few small businessmen ever to serve in the White House."

He reminded us that one of his initiatives—easing regulatory burdens and paperwork while getting rid of overlapping and obsolete rules—was making good progress. This, in fact, was an area that I'm proud to have worked on with the administration early in my tenure with the Small Business Council. I told the Chamber at the outset that I wanted to focus on two areas: the pre-interstate banking system and international trade. Both were in great need of repair, but none more than the antiquated banking situation and its resulting negative impact on small business.

In essence, existing regulations prevented a businessman from borrowing money in one area and putting it to use in another. In my case for example, a bank in Tampa couldn't loan me money to become a dealer 45 miles away in Lakeland. The problem during this period was that businesses were outpacing the banks. Think of it this way: In 1976, the average price of a used car on a dealer's lot was $1,200, meaning that $120,000 would equate to 100 used cars. But all of a sudden, the price of a used car increased to closer to $10,000. If you do the math, that means you now needed a million dollars for an inventory of 100 cars. The problem was that the banks didn't have $1 million to lend you, creating a potentially crippling problem for many small industries, including ours. You simply could not grow in that environment. I recognized this, which is why I requested the opportunity to work on the interstate banking issue, determined to find a solution.

Because we had so many small banks with limited resources, there wasn't enough available capital to support small businesses in a position to grow. The regulations prevented large banks such as Citibank and Chase from stepping in to lend capital to a company wanting to expand across state lines. One side-effect of my heavy involvement in this issue: Citibank asked that I speak to a banker and Fordham professor who was authoring a book on the problem, entitled Access To Capital. I wound up writing the foreword.

Two top officials for Citibank/Citicorp—CEO Walter Wriston and chairman John Reed—asked for my help with a simmering problem in Florida. SunBank was fighting restrictions on interstate banking that were blocking its effort to merge with the Trust Company of Georgia. Eventually, my work with the administration in my Small Business Council role led to passage of new legislation that made interstate banking possible. The upshot in Florida: SunBank merged with the Trust Company of Georgia, forming the large banking chain we know as SunTrust.

It marked the first time that a bank was allowed to buy a trust company and, in the big picture, the legislation allowing interstate banking opened up the whole banking industry across the United States. Banks were now in a position to help companies expand their presence in various parts of the country—and larger banks with more funding ability could play an unfettered role in that process.

That's basically how I first lent a hand on the public-policy front. I'm proud of the positive effects of my efforts—helping small businesses grow and gain higher visibility, and helping areas like Tampa Bay become less insulated from a business perspective and more growth-oriented. It's my view that the advent of interstate banking changed the business climate in the United States forever.

Sam Gibbons was very supportive of this as well. Sam was a Democrat and we disagreed on many things, but we always had a very good relationship and he taught me a lot. Without a doubt, this change in banking helped my own business. I would not have been able to take any significant steps forward under the old banking system.

Meanwhile, I had my hands full with other pressing issues in my leadership capacity with the Chamber. I worked with local, state and national business groups to advocate for the passage of the Capital Cost Recovery Act, designed to promote investment in state-of-the-art tools and equipment as a means of increasing productivity.

Working on initiatives with the Carter Administration occasionally put us in the midst of world events. In March 1979, the President was engaged in brokering peace talks between Israeli Prime Minister Menachem Begin and Egyptian President Anwar Sadat, when the two Middle East leaders came to Washington. We attended a luncheon for Prime Minister Begin, hosted by the U.S. Chamber of Commerce and the Israel-U.S. Business Council. There was also a dinner hosted by the Chamber and the Egypt-U.S. Business Council in honor of President Sadat, introduced by my friend and talented colleague Dr. Richard

Lesher, who would serve a remarkable 22 years as President of the U.S. Chamber of Commerce. Given the historic backdrop of the talks, it was genuinely exciting to hear the three principal players—Carter, Begin and Sadat—talk about bridging differences in the name of peace. Carol even got to know Mrs. Sadat a little and thought she was charming. The experiences added to our deep sadness two years later when President Sadat was assassinated for negotiating peace with Israel.

On the domestic front, Supreme Court Chief Justice Warren E. Burger, who was a huge advocate of prison industries, formed a committee on the subject in the early 1980s—the Prison Industries Council—and I was asked to participate. During that period, another issue began to demand my attention. With import sales on the rise nationally, domestic auto manufacturers responded by imploring the White House to place quotas on imports. That would obviously have been devastating to me and other import dealers around the country. I argued vigorously against this possibility as Chairman of the Small Business Council, repeatedly making the point that failing dealerships—regardless of whether they are domestic or import—are unhealthy for our economy. "There are certain things you risk in a free enterprise system," I said. "You have the opportunity to make a profit or you have the potential to go broke." I was one of many voices urging the administration not to impose quotas, stating that the price of cars would soar, oil consumption for less economical cars would rise and consumers would lose. We were delighted that President Carter refused to impose quotas.

About this time, the reigning president of the U.S. Chamber of Commerce, William K. Eastman, a conservationist passionate about preserving the duck population, stepped down. I was asked to speak at his sendoff and present him with a beautiful, carved replica of a duck. I used the opportunity to liken ducks to the inherent traits of small business.

"First, the duck is essentially a swimming bird. However, like a small businessman, the duck can fly when given an opportunity. Or he can walk on solid ground. Or he can dive.

"By land, sea or air, he can retreat or move forward as conditions warrant.

"The duck finds himself a frequent target—not unlike small businesses."

Then, to complete the metaphor, I added, "The duck makes a lot of noise. And when it does, it is not a pretty sound, but it is unmistakable. More small business people need to make noise."

People have described me as calm and unassuming in my personal style, but I had no trouble making noise for the cause of small business. Sometimes, I made noise when the topic was chickens, not ducks. Case in point: my testimony before Congress about a ridiculously outdated development on the international trade front: the "Chicken Tax" on pickup trucks. It dates back to 1966 when Germany put a tax on chickens imported from the United States. At that time, Germany—via Volkswagen—was exporting a fair number of pickups to the United States. So we retaliated by placing a tax on the pickups. Unfortunately, no amount of common-sense arguments prevailed. And to this day, every pickup truck made in Japan, Korea or Europe has an automatic 25 percent tax attached to it if it's exported to the U.S—and it's called the Chicken Tax.

Meanwhile, in Tampa, business continued to blossom. The six dealerships I owned were doing a healthy annual sales volume and the American International Automobile Dealers Association selected me from a group of 4,500 U.S. import dealers as the Outstanding Import Motorcar Dealer in the United States. Life was so busy from my travel for the Chamber of Commerce—including treasurer duties as well—that I had to resign from several boards. But I still served on the Board of Trustees for the University of Tampa and St. Joseph's Hospital and was honored to receive the President's Distinguished Citizen Award from the University of South Florida.

This was also a time of change. Our daughters had grown up, attended college and gotten married, Leann to Mike Rowe and Suzy to Lawrence Anderson. But there was also change on the national stage, as Ronald Reagan defeated Carter in the landslide election of Nov. 5, 1980. I actually had raised money for George Bush during the campaign. But that didn't stop President Reagan from appointing me to the Small Business Administrative Advisory Council, a post I held for the first four years of his administration. I spent a good deal of time in Reagan's presence as well as members of his cabinet and officials from regulatory agencies. I continued to fly in my personal plane throughout the country, giving speeches with a simple message: that one man can make a difference and it's important for all of us to get involved in the process, pushing for whatever we feel is right.

One of the nicest compliments I received during this phase came in a letter from the U.S. Chamber of Commerce that read:

"It would be difficult to overstate the contribution that Frank Morsani has made to Small Business in America through his leadership of the Council of Small Business of the U.S. Chamber of Commerce.

"We are long past counting the hours he has spent or the miles he has traveled to work for business in every part of the United States.

"As a result, he may be more widely recognized across the country than in Tampa as a small business leader. His contribution is composed also of a mixture of modesty and self-confidence with which he approaches life. On the one hand, he instinctively treats the so-called ordinary people around him with respect and consideration. He is just as likely to look at a

Cabinet Secretary or the President in the eye and say what he thinks.

"What he thinks is nearly always sound, while being practical about what individuals in groups can do to help small business.

"What Frank Morsani has contributed most is that quality we call leadership, the rare capacity to transmit life and vitality into a group, to help members of the group develop a feeling of common purpose. Over the years he has gained the deep respect of his colleagues on the Chamber's Board of Directors and the loyalty of the members of the council."

I was moved by those kind sentiments and immensely honored when the 65-member Board of Directors elected me in 1984 as Vice Chairman of the Board of the U.S. Chamber of Commerce, the traditional first step to becoming Chairman of the Board the following year. My life had been filled with so much good fortune—from the love and support of Carol and the children to being named a finalist by Time magazine in its 1983 Quality Dealer Awards for the success of my business. Much to my surprise, I was also named by Florida's Democratic Governor, Bob Graham, to the Hillsborough County Aviation Authority's five-person board of directors in '83.

Carol still enjoys telling the story of how that happened. "We were on vacation in Venice, Italy and sitting on the patio of our hotel, sipping cocktails and getting ready to take a little boat ride to the storied Vecchia Murano Glass Factory. Suddenly, someone walked out of the hotel and said, 'There's a long-distance call for you. It turned out it was from Bob Graham's senior counsel, offering Frank the Aviation Authority job. I was hacked! We're in the middle of vacation and they can't leave us alone for dinner?"

It was definitely a unique setting in which to receive such an honor. I served for eight years, eventually becoming chairman, and I'm proud of what we accomplished in that time:

opening two new airsides, including the addition of bustling Airside A, and helping Tampa International Airport continue to grow into one of the country's model airports.

Two years after joining the Aviation Authority, I was gratified that Governor Graham appointed me in 1985 to the Florida Council of 100, a private, non-partisan, non-profit group of business leaders dedicated to working with the Governor on promoting statewide economic growth. In the meantime, I had added such new dealerships as Precision Isuzu, Ford and Mercury in Carson City, Nev., Precision Leasing in the Bay Area and Winter Haven Chrysler-Plymouth-Dodge, helping to increase sales to $130 million.

Yet becoming the Chamber's Chair was hard to top. The organization had a budget of $60 million, with 1,300 full-time employees and more than 240,000 members, along with 28 standing committees. It was especially gratifying to learn that I was one of only two Floridians ever elected to the position. But the most extraordinary part of the job was the travel that took us far away from Florida—giving speeches in such places as Milan, Rome, Bonn, Geneva, Frankfurt, Hangzhou, Shanghai, and Beijing. In Venice, I attended a large symposium that dealt with the many problems facing Italy. Government leaders from all over the country packed the hall to hear me talk about entrepreneurialism and American business; I think every official from the country was there except the Pope. In 1985, I had the opportunity to serve as the keynote speaker in Edinburgh, Scotland before the board chairmen of the world's major oil companies.

The audiences were always keenly interested in what America was doing and I thoroughly enjoyed serving as a conduit of the United States business community—specifically from the perspective of small business as opposed to a multi-national corporation. It was certainly a long way from my formative years in Detroit writing service manuals, or my years driving through north Florida as a master mechanic for Ford. Back then, I never could have imagined that one day I'd be jetting around the world addressing foreign dignitaries.

The best part was that Carol and I got to experience the travel together. The officials hosting us would take us on spectacular tours of their cities, seeing the famous sights with no shortage of fine dinners along the way. Occasionally, the trips would overlap with dealership work as well, with visits by Carol and me to various import manufacturing plants to get a better sense of the production process. It was truly the best of both worlds, seeing countries and their cultures in a new light and doing a little car business, too. And there was an added bonus. While traveling or shopping with Carol abroad, I learned what new trends in color and style were on the horizon and that proved helpful in anticipating consumer-purchasing decisions at my dealerships.

One of my more memorable moments overseas came in early October 1985 when I had the opportunity to give a speech at the center of Dutch government, the Hague. I addressed a group that consisted of the American Chamber of Commerce in the Netherlands—one of our 53 overseas affiliates—and the Super Task Force to Internationalize the Tampa Bay Area. My talk was about trade and business in the United States, and the *St. Petersburg Times* carried this dateline report: "In a speech the Dutch business people found sobering and Tampa Bay business people hailed as 'hard-hitting,' the Chairman of the U.S. Chamber of Commerce called for shutting countries out of U.S. markets if they are shutting U.S. traders out of their markets. Overall, though, the speaker, Tampa auto dealer Frank Morsani, strongly condemned protectionist bills before Congress as 'false solutions—measures that will do more harm than good.' "

On this occasion in the Netherlands, Prime Minister Ruud Lubbers was in attendance, and he later invited me to his office to talk more about business opportunities. The meeting gave me an opening to broach a topic that was "off the books." When feasible, the administration wanted me to speak to foreign government officials about housing anti-ballistic missiles, in response to concerns about the Soviet Union's ability to launch missile strikes against Europe. My unofficial agenda, on behalf of the U.S. government, was to discuss with Prime Minister Lubbers the possibility of having America install ABMs in the Netherlands. He was receptive, opening the door for the White House to follow up. This was not an isolated experience. Very often, if the President was planning a trip to a certain country, and I already happened to be scheduled to speak there on behalf of the Chamber, I might be contacted by administration officials. They'd ask me to scope out certain business issues and provide input that could be helpful to the President when he arrived.

Less than two weeks after leaving the Netherlands, Carol and I embarked on the trip of a lifetime: a 10-day visit to China that allowed me to meet with the nation's leaders and explore the possibility of forming a closer relationship with American business. Our arrival came on the heels of warming relations with the superpower. Only four months earlier, Chinese President Li Xiannian had come to Washington, where he and President Reagan had signed a nuclear cooperation agreement and undertaken new cultural and educational exchanges.

When we arrived in China in mid-October, Carol and I were supposed to stay in Premier Zhao Ziyang's guesthouse, but our hosts apologetically explained that we had to be bumped to make way for two other guests, Vice President George Bush and his wife, Barbara, who had come for the opening of the U.S. Consulate General in Chengdu. We laughed—obviously Carol and I had no complaints whatsoever about moving to another room. It was the start of an amazing trip. We traveled to Beijing and down to Hangzhou, then to Shanghai, holding fascinating and productive talks each stop along the way—including a meeting with Li Peng, China's newly appointed Minister of the State Education Commission, and future leader of the country.

This was the period in China when the country was bringing back exiled officials, many of whom spoke fluent English. One of the men we met had been educated at MIT and was now serving on the All China Federation of Commerce and Industry—just one of many highly successful business people we encountered, including a woman who ran a steel company in Shanghai. All were in their 70s and 80s and returning from exile. The job of these impressive individuals was to help organize China's business community, something very exciting to observe. And it was thrilling to know that we were among the first representatives of U.S. business to travel to China after the country opened up to the West.

At this point in the country's history, the streets were still devoid of automobiles—other than the few that were operated by government officials. Bicyclists jammed the busy thoroughfares of the cities as the dominant form of transportation. Instead of panel trucks, you'd see bicycles equipped with platforms on the back to haul fruits, vegetables and even small refrigerators. Beijing was very different from the booming metropolis that would one day host the 2008 Summer Olympics, with no grass or greenery to speak of anywhere in the city. We were told that the loss of greenery had been caused by sparrow eradication campaigns launched by Communist Chinese Chairman Mao Zedong from 1958-62—part of an effort to improve health and hygiene to decrease the risk of spreading disease. This, however, created a devastating ecological chain-reaction that resulted in locust infestations, which, in turn, led to massive deforestation.

Throughout our stay, we were invited to one banquet after the next, and the food often posed a challenge to our taste buds. "I remember one dinner," Carol says, "they brought out turtle soup, which tasted pretty good—until we noticed a dead turtle, shell and all, floating in the big bowl. The guest of honor got the shell—luckily, that wasn't us!" In spite of cuisine that could induce such queasiness—including side dishes of sea slugs—we truly count ourselves fortunate to have experienced China then, giving us an amazing point of comparison for the country's surging modernization in recent decades.

It was and is a vivid example of what travel affords you as a window into other cultures—and a reminder of how fortunate we are to live in a country founded on personal freedom and opportunity. Only four years after our visit, the Chinese government—now run by the official we had met, Premier Li Peng—crushed protests by pro-democracy students and demonstrators in the Tiananmen Square Massacre of June 1989. It was sad to see such a tragedy unfold against the backdrop of the China we had encountered, yet in keeping with the country's historic pattern of opening itself up to Western influences for brief periods—and then abruptly pushing them away.

Several years after our visit, another landmark event occurred on the world stage that involved the U.S. Chamber of Commerce. When East Germany opened up the Berlin Wall on Nov. 9, 1989, a half-dozen ambassadors from Eastern European countries came to the United States the very next day, and we held a dinner for them at the State Department to discuss business opportunities. It was such a privilege to connect with these foreign officials who were eager to finally establish a business relationship with the U.S.

On occasion, world leaders came for visits to the United States and I acted as their host. One week, I escorted Indian Prime Minister Rajiv Gandhi around Washington, D.C. and to a series of business meetings. He was India's youngest prime minister, an impressive man who came to power in 1984 after the assassination of his mother, Prime Minister Indira Gandhi. In keeping with tradition of visiting heads of state, Rajiv Gandhi held a dinner in Washington before returning home, and we were in attendance—just as we were at similar dinners for Turkey's Prime Minister Turgut Özal and other foreign leaders. We also attended White House dinners to honor dignitaries from abroad, like the glitzy gala in October 1985 for Singapore's Prime Minister Lee Kuan Yu. The guest list included such names as Sylvester Stallone and his future wife Brigitte Nielsen, singer Natalie Cole, TV and film actor Michael J. Fox and actress Raquel Welch. Carol remembers that night well:

"Frank was at a table with Secretary of State George Schultz and Raquel Welch. They're trying to talk—and she's in the middle of them going on about how lovely she is. They always separate husbands and wives for dinner seating at these affairs, so I was at another table with Natalie Cole and Robert McFarlane. He was the retired National Security Advisor—the man, we later learned, who had secretly carried a cake baked in the shape of a key to Iranian leaders to symbolize an opening of improved relations between the two countries. Frank's table was near the front and we were all the way in the back, but at least Barbara Bush came by my table and complimented my black velvet dress. She was so kind and down to earth."

Having the chance to work with Presidents Carter, Reagan, and Bush was truly amazing for an old car mechanic like me. Carol and I had dinner with Mr. and Mrs. Bush several times, just the four of us. They're wonderful people. I attended many White House meetings with President Reagan, and my impression was that he was very sharp during his first term, but in his second term would occasionally lose his train of thought. Though I'd supported Bush in 1980, Reagan gained my admiration when I participated in meetings with him and saw him to be well-prepared and very articulate. He knew what he was talking about and he knew how to listen: When he ran for his second term, I was glad I could help by flying his daughter,

Maureen, all over Florida and Georgia in my plane during the campaign.

I also attended a great many meetings with President Carter. When his administration was preparing to put the wage and price controls in place, I'd go to Washington every other week and spend time in the old Executive Office Building with Carter's "inflation czar" and Chairman of Wage and Price stability, Alfred Kahn—the man who had deregulated the airlines. We'd sit in rocking chairs and discuss the wage and price issue and gradually became friends. I don't know if my conversations with him had any effect, but my side won. They never enacted the legislation.

It was difficult to have a personal meeting with Carter. Whether it was four people or more, one of them would always be the First Lady, Rosalynn; he never would have a meeting without her being present. To be honest, that ticked a lot of people off. It was hard to feel you could talk to the President about something really important with his wife sitting in the corner. In addition, he was a micromanager of the worst order.

My own style with the Chamber was to try to quietly build coalitions in order to achieve a desired result. The Chamber employed 20 fulltime lobbyists, making us one of the nation's most powerful lobby groups—taking an active role in more than 100 issues the year I became chairman. Rather than wait for Congress to pass a piece of legislation, the Chamber was now attempting to influence legislation before it was even introduced—often reinforcing our efforts with highly orchestrated letter-writing campaigns aimed at U.S. representatives.

As I mentioned, my style with dealership employees was similarly low-key and inclusive. But I was tough when it came to enforcing our anti-drug policy in the workplace, instituting a creative approach to deal with a problem that was increasingly widespread in the '70s and '80s. We were wasting a lot of money testing employees for drugs, and one day I had an idea of how to eliminate that cost. I decided to charge every applicant $50 when undergoing a physical. If you paid your money and passed your physical, we'd give you your money back. That essentially eliminated the drug problem in our company, because nobody wanted to throw away $50.

I wound up with people who took their jobs seriously and I rewarded them accordingly. But my intrinsic belief about the benefits that come from hard work, from treating people with respect and honesty, was severely challenged by another formative experience during this period of business success.

In 1983, I was approached by members of the Tampa sports and business community to lead an organization dedicated to bringing Major League Baseball to Tampa. For years, Pinellas and Hillsborough Counties had competed for the opportunity to land a big-league team and bring it to their respective side of the bay. I had never been a particular fan of the game. There hadn't been time in my life as a youth to develop an attachment to a baseball team or play the sport. But I understood the economic impact a major league franchise would have on the city and region, and I believed I could help get the job done. So I gladly accepted the position as President of the Tampa Bay Baseball Group.

A story in my hometown newspaper, the *Tampa Tribune*, explained our goal: to clear the long-standing minor league facility, Al Lopez Field, on Dale Mabry Highway in September 1983, and then—after the area's first Super Bowl was held on Jan. 23, 1984—start construction on a major league baseball stadium. I'd served as a board member of the baseball group and took over from architect Ray Bennett, who had been an organizer and promoter in the early stages of the endeavor. The consensus was that a new leader with business experience was now needed to help the baseball dream come true for Tampa.

But it didn't take long to recognize the fine line between dream and nightmare.

CHAPTER NINE

Betrayed by Baseball

My life in the early 1980s was busy and rewarding, and I certainly didn't need a new project to be personally or professionally fulfilled. But the prospect of bringing baseball to Tampa, a city on the rise and a place that Carol and I had come to love, was too intriguing to ignore. Simply stated, it was a good economic fit for our community, and all the pieces seemed to be falling together to make a viable run at America's grand old game. Florida had the tradition, through decades of spring training in the state. We had the local business clout and dollars to court baseball. And we had the vision to make it happen.

The story of what ultimately took place in this quest was too painful for me to dwell on in the aftermath. I couldn't even read a sports page for two years—there were too many stinging reminders of what occurred with Major League Baseball. That's history now. We've handled it and moved on with our lives. But the lessons we learned are worth sharing—about how the game of baseball is played at the top echelons, about the depth of civic divisions that separated Tampa and St. Petersburg, and about the need to keep persevering in the darkest of days.

This is the tale of what took place, leaving a trail of broken promises and more than a few broken hearts along the way. My intention here isn't to relate every twist and turn in the road that eventually led to the arrival of big-league baseball in Tampa Bay; there are far too many to cover. But this is how the game played out while I was involved, giving everything I could muster—in commitment of time, energy and millions of dollars—trying to land a major league team for my hometown.

The seeds of my involvement were planted in 1982. Up until that point, St. Petersburg and the Pinellas County Sports Authority had been taking the lead in the push for baseball. The most likely location for a proposed stadium to house a team was the Gateway area of Pinellas County, a spot in north St. Petersburg at the edge of the Howard Frankland Bridge and just across the bay from Tampa. The location made perfect sense—it would be easily accessible from St. Petersburg, nearby Clearwater and Tampa, and the surrounding cities comprising the Tampa Bay region. For three years, Orlando architect Ray Bennett worked with the Pinellas Sports Authority in promoting the wide-open, industrial Gateway site to build a ballpark.

But in the summer of '82, the Pinellas Sports Authority switched its sights to a tract of land in downtown St. Petersburg, a stretch of low-income homes on land that had once housed a gas plant. The "Gas Plant" site came with a highly affordable price tag and a plan to finance a domed stadium—the roof being a must for Florida's stormy summers—with public dollars. The less central location also fractured alliances. Ray broke from the Pinellas group and met with New York Yankees owner George Steinbrenner and Tampa mayor Bob Martinez, who convinced him that he should try to bring a major league team to Tampa. That got the ball rolling, along with stalwart media support from longtime *Tampa Tribune* sports editor and my good friend Tom McEwen.

Before long, Ed McGinty, an attorney who had done work for Tampa's Downtown Development Authority, came on board and other key players were joining the newly formed Tampa Bay Baseball Group. One of them, Bob Humphries, was my lawyer, and he invited me on a spur-of-the-moment trip to Hawaii to attend a party arranged by George Steinbrenner at the Baseball Winter Meetings. Many influential people would be in attendance and Bob felt my presence could help the group move forward. Several years later, Bob reflected on the events in a *Tampa Tribune* story, saying, "We were looking for a leader, a doer. (Frank) did his own independent research and concurred that this was an economic opportunity that shouldn't be overlooked."

Meanwhile, Tom McEwen urged me to take an active role, and introduced me to the Tribune's editorial page editor, Edwin Roberts. He was a huge baseball fan and expressed his belief in the enormous value that a big-league team would have for Tampa, suggesting I play a role in the process. Mayor Martinez had already paved the way for an important initial step, helping the group negotiate a lease for Al Lopez Field. The old ballpark on well-traveled Dale Mabry Highway was the spring training base of the Cincinnati Reds and only several blocks from Tampa Stadium, the National Football League home of the expansion Tampa Bay Buccaneers. We were convinced that the area was ripe for baseball and burgeoning Tampa was its most favorable location.

When I accepted the group's offer to become its president, I had one stipulation: I would take on the responsibility only if I could get some other key people to work with me. That was no issue.

I engaged Joe Casper, who owned some two-dozen McDonald's franchises in the area and could lend expertise on concessions. There was Ed Winton, the owner of several radio stations, who could bring a valuable perspective on broadcasts and communications. Hotel owner Ted Couch joined, providing hospitality experience. And I got a lot of local people into the mix with a variety of strengths. We all wrote $25,000 checks and moved forward.

But what we needed now was a financial heavy hitter. None of us had the kind of money it would take to buy a baseball team—costing give or take $50 million. That role could be played by Bill Mack, who owned the office center called the Mack Building in downtown Tampa. The Mack family was formidable, owning several million square feet of prime office space in northern New Jersey, just across the Hudson River from Manhattan. The father, H. Bert Mack, wintered in Palm Beach and Bill was one of his three sons. Given the sizeable net worth the Mack's purportedly had, we reached out to them to be our deep pockets—and Bill agreed to get involved, represented by his attorney, Jim Cusack.

We also enlisted the support of a highly respected, veteran baseball executive, Cedric Tallis. Cedric gave us the kind of credibility we needed with baseball owners and leadership. He'd spent more than 40 years in baseball, had been the Yankees' general manager the previous eight seasons for George Steinbrenner and was ready to retire. I went to George, who obviously knew what we were doing, and asked if he minded if we hired Cedric. The Boss gladly gave the move his blessing. Cedric knew everyone in baseball—and I say everyone, because I eventually met with most of them myself: the presidents of the American and National Leagues, several commissioners and a whole array of those characters.

In short order, our prospects began to look quite promising in our parallel pursuit of either an existing franchise or a future expansion team. We outbid another group's offer on the Al Lopez site, signing a 75-year lease with the Tampa Sports Authority. That cleared the way for the stadium we intended to build with private financing, unlike what we regarded as the ill-advised publicly funded project in St. Petersburg.

Then came news that aging Minnesota Twins owner Calvin Griffith had expressed interest in selling his team to our group. Minnesota had the poorest attendance in the American League, a fact that irritated fellow owners because they received 20 percent of the gate revenues and were losing money—and patience—with the Twins. Unfortunately, our negotiations with Mr. Griffith fell apart after several months, but we found ourselves back in the game in April 1984.

A minority owner of the Twins, Gabe Murphy, expressed interest to us in selling his 42.14-percent share. He had made his money in insurance and lived in Washington, D.C., so Jim Cusack and I flew to the nation's capital to meet with him. I even brought along a Key Lime pie for him and his wife. We sat in their house and made a deal to buy Mr. Murphy's percent share for about $50 million, which gave us controlling interest of the franchise—owning the largest slice of the proverbial Key Lime pie. It looked like we had hit a home run right out of the box.

But that's where things began to get dicey. Soon after we made the purchase, Commissioner Bowie Kuhn made it clear that baseball was not going to approve any deal to buy the Twins and move them to Tampa. This completely caught us off guard. Everybody in baseball had been saying Florida should have a team, and they'd made their displeasure with Minnesota as a location eminently clear. We felt we could move the team and if they really wanted to keep baseball in Minneapolis, they could eventually put an expansion team there down the road.

But Kuhn, along with American League president Bobby Brown, refused to consider that scenario. We were given two choices: either sell our stock back to Murphy, or sell our interest at cost to a prominent Minnesota banker, Carl Pohlad. They dangled this carrot: If we sold our interest to Pohlad, who also owned a Pepsi Cola distributorship in Fort Myers and Pensacola, we would be rewarded with an expansion team. They wouldn't allow us to make any money on the new transaction, even though the price had gone up considerably during the time we'd purchased the shares. We agreed with a handshake to their demand, but only on the basis that we would get the next available team. We were assured that would be the case, so we played ball with Bowie and decided to focus our efforts going forward on expansion.

But expansion was still firmly on baseball's back burner. And in the meantime, more opportunities arose to negotiate with existing teams. We received a call from the Oakland Athletics, who apparently had concluded that the San Francisco Bay Area wasn't going to support two major league franchises in the A's and Giants. They expressed to me that they wanted to sell the team and work with us to move the club to Tampa. I set up a meeting, flew to Dallas and spoke with the son of denim jeans magnate Levi Strauss—the chairman of the board of the A's, as well as his brother-in-law, a banker with Citibank in San Francisco. I asked if they really wanted to sell, and they said they were fed up with the City of Oakland, the lack of financial support and a subpar stadium. So we drew up a contract, once again shelling out many thousands of dollars on legal costs. Then several of us—including Carol—flew to San Francisco to start the ball rolling.

We attended the 1984 All-Star Game at Candlestick Park and afterwards I met with the top brass of the Athletics. Our talks went so smoothly that we struck a deal on the spot and, much to our astonishment, signed an agreement to buy the A's. Who would have guessed we'd have hit the jackpot so quickly after the Twins disappointment? Our group flew home to Tampa, giddy over the fast-moving events but careful to keep the deal quiet until it could be formally announced. At about 4 p.m., shortly after arriving at our house, I received a call from one of Oakland's front-office officials who told me, "We're going to have a press conference in Oakland and announce that you've purchased our team, but we don't want you to say anything until you've heard it from us."

That was fine, because I knew we had a signed contract. The next morning, I received a call from the same official, assuming it was to give me the go-ahead to make our announcement. "Well, we've worked everything out with Oakland and we're staying here," he said in a matter-of-fact tone. I was momentarily speechless, absorbing the unexpected blow before asking what happened. Overnight, Oakland mayor Lionel Wilson had given the A's a grant for $10 million to revamp their stadium if they stayed. We could have sued, but we had no guarantee of winning. And if we'd have lost what could have become a prolonged, expensive, cross-country suit, we'd have burned our bridges with baseball. Our Tampa group had been nothing but a "stalking horse" for all those folks with the A's to get exactly what they wanted.

But we dusted ourselves off and, soon enough, another opportunity arose in the form of the Seattle Mariners. Their owner, George Argyros, was reportedly growing increasingly unhappy with terrible attendance for his club and wanted to speak to me about selling the Mariners to our group. He insisted on having the meeting outside the United States, to minimize the chances of word leaking out to the media. He had business in London, and asked if I could meet him there. It seemed like a worthwhile shot, so I agreed, booked a flight and arranged to meet Mr. Argyros at the Churchill Hotel. Long story short: No deal materialized from our discussions, but a two-fold trend was becoming clear: a) teams struggling with attendance wanted to speak to us; and b) the game's power brokers talked as if they wanted different ownership in place for those clubs, consistently praising the Tampa Bay Baseball Group as a good fit for Major League Baseball.

At one point or another, almost all the key baseball people visited me in my office to encourage us. Cedric Tallis, myself and a handful of others attended several baseball owners' meetings a year. I was even asked to stand up in various sessions, where they'd proclaim to the gathering, "These are the people we want to have Major League Baseball."

Furthermore, we appeared to have the edge in the eyes of baseball's ruling powers when it came to our neighbor across the bay, St. Petersburg. There's no question in my mind—and in the opinion of many others—that our active pursuit of a team forced the pro-stadium backers on the Pinellas side of the bridge to accelerate their plans to build a domed stadium on the Gas Plant land. They were pinning all their hopes on the old Field of Dreams philosophy—if you build it they will come. But they were building it at taxpayers' expense and that was simply not a desirable option for our group. What's more, the new baseball commissioner, Peter Ueberroth, left no doubt where he stood in 1986 on St. Pete's big gamble of constructing the Florida Suncoast Dome without a team in place.

He asked George Steinbrenner, Co-Chairman of the Long Range Planning Committee, to inform St. Pete officials involved with the dome plans that building the indoor ballpark would not improve their chances for landing a franchise and, to the contrary, might actually damage them. When an editorial in the *St. Petersburg Times* characterized Steinbrenner as "a dubious messenger of baseball," Ueberroth issued a direct message to the Mayor of St. Petersburg, Edward L. Cole Jr. He wrote in a telegram: "Indeed, in our evaluation of potential cities for relocation or expansion, St. Petersburg is not among the top candidates."

We understood that St. Petersburg's low standing didn't automatically mean we were high on the list. But we certainly felt good about our chances in light of Ueberroth's message, especially when you factored in all the positive comments made to us by baseball leaders. We also engineered a political victory in Washington, D.C. during 1986 that appeared to level the playing field between Tampa and St. Petersburg in construction costs. We went to Capitol Hill—thanks to an inside connection our attorney, Jim Cusack, had with the powerful Ways and Means Committee—and helped win the right to use the same kind of tax-free development bonds that St. Petersburg was utilizing in its construction of the dome. We literally accomplished this in a hallway of Congress with a group of attorneys—I was the only non-lawyer in the bunch. The upshot: St. Pete no longer held an advantage over our group in financing construction of the stadium.

In an interview with the *Tampa Tribune*, I re-stated our position that St. Petersburg's move to build a stadium had no impact on our stadium plans. "I'm sticking right by what I've said all along. If the good folks of Pinellas County have decided to spend their money in that manner, that's their business. We will proceed on the same course we have all along. Our financing is in place and we are going ahead with the same plans we have had all along."

Many people don't know that in 1987 we nearly made a second successful attempt to buy the Minnesota Twins, whose poor attendance continued to drag the franchise down. But the Twins won the '87 World Series, revitalized their attendance and the deal never materialized. A year later, however, things began to heat up on multiple fronts, eventually reaching a boiling point. The National League had been making some noise about adding two more franchises, and in 1988 members of the U.S. Senate threatened to revoke baseball's antitrust exemption if the sport didn't move faster to expand. Naturally, we viewed that as a very encouraging development.

Then there was the near coup that the St. Petersburg forces nearly pulled off, negotiating with Chicago White Sox owner Jerry Reinsdorf to move his team to St. Pete for the start of the 1989 season. Reinsdorf even agreed to a 15-year lease to play in the Suncoast Dome. A wave of excitement swept through the area as the entire deal hung on a late-night session of the Illinois legislature, which had a chance to stop the move if it approved

funding before midnight for a new stadium to replace deterio-
rating Comiskey Park. By all accounts, there weren't enough
votes to prevent the White Sox from coming to Florida. But
based on my experience to date, I suspected that St. Petersburg
was being played by baseball—in this case, by one of its most
powerful owners, Reinsdorf—just the way we had been used by
the A's in an attempt to get a better stadium deal in Oakland.

Countless people in Tampa Bay watched on live television
as Illinois governor Jim Thompson walked the floor of the legislature, changing one vote after the next before the midnight
deadline—and, amazingly, they even stopped the clock before
12 a.m. so he could twist more arms! I guess that was an example of Chicago politics in action. By the time Thompson
was done, the vote had changed from certain celebration in St.
Pete to stunned silence as the legislature approved a new White
Sox stadium after all.

The fact is, I had begun talks with new St. Petersburg Mayor
Bob Ulrich to explore ways we might patch up our differences,
a scenario that increasingly seemed to be the message from Ueberroth. Our Tampa Bay Baseball Group was even considering
the previously unthinkable possibility of placing any team we
might land in St. Pete's emerging dome. It was during this period that—after a monumental investment of time and money—
we finally appeared to have landed the elusive prize.

Out of the blue, we received a call that Texas Rangers owner
Eddie Chiles wanted to sell his 58-percent controlling interest
in his franchise. Chiles had made his money with an oil-drill-
ing service company he owned, Western Oil, and was a popular
figure in Dallas. He even had his own radio show. Rangers attendance had plunged and Chiles was running out of money
to make payroll, so he had no choice but to seek a buyer for
his franchise. We spoke with his chief operating officer long
enough to get the full picture. Before we engaged in any serious talks, however, I wanted an assurance from baseball that

we weren't simply walking down the same dead end path we'd followed with the Twins and A's.

I set up an appointment with Ueberroth's office and called Bill Mack so he could accompany me. We flew to New York and sat down with the commissioner in his spacious midtown Manhattan office. The first thing Ueberroth told us was, "This meeting never took place"—as if to signal that whatever thumbs up he'd be giving us was only for our benefit. I sat across from him and said, "Look, we've been a stalking horse for baseball long enough. Do you want us to buy the Texas Rangers? And if we do, are you going to approve the deal or are you just stroking us?"

Ueberroth responded without missing a beat, assuring us that he was glad we were buying the team. I should add that, years later, when he was asked about it, he denied ever telling us this. But I assure you that he did. It was an odd meeting, because he informed us that he'd have to leave briefly for a press conference downstairs to announce that he was stepping down as commissioner before the 1989 season. That's how I know what date our meeting took place—June 7, 1988.

In any event, Ueberroth's blessing of our plan to purchase the Rangers was all we needed to hear. I proceeded to spend more than a half-million dollars on attorneys and certified public accountants from Deloitte & Touche, which brought in its top entertainment industry CPAs. With their assistance, we fashioned a contract and entered into serious discussions to buy the Rangers. This was an amazing and unexpected turn of events, when you consider Chiles and his representatives had been searching all over Dallas—home to no shortage of wealthy businessmen –to find new owners for the team. But none had emerged, which explains why

Ueberroth had no objections to our out-of-state group making the purchase.

Cedric Tallis—our ace-in-the-hole baseball man—and I evaluated every ballplayer the Rangers had under contract, both in the majors and the minors. There were about 200 of them in all. Veteran baseball guys like Cedric could recognize talent as if it was a science. I wouldn't know it if it hit me in the face. But with Cedric's expert eye, we ranked the Rangers personnel top to bottom. I made multiple trips over the next few months to Dallas, visiting Chiles at his beautiful home in Fort Worth and being interviewed—in some cases, grilled—by the hometown media.

For the record, Bill Mack and I decided to make the $85 million purchase independent of the Tampa Bay Baseball Group, making us the official co-owners of the club. This simply seemed like the most expedient way to orchestrate the deal, but naturally, the Dallas-Fort Worth press viewed us with suspicion. I explained our position every time I was asked: We were not necessarily going to move the Rangers to Tampa. It was possible that we could leave them in Arlington if baseball guaranteed that we would receive one of the anticipated expansion teams, and then sell the Rangers to owners who would keep them in Texas. The other scenario was that baseball could approve moving the Rangers to Tampa—perhaps even playing in St. Pete's dome—and promise to replace them with an expansion team in Texas.

Now I should point out that Carol was not in favor of our pursuit of the franchise, in light of how we'd been burned previously. But we forged ahead. As we worked out the details of the deal, we were still unsure about where the franchise would be located—we wanted to do what was best for baseball. After three months of talks, we flew Chiles to Tampa, wined and dined him at the Harbour Island Hotel, and handed him a check to buy the Rangers. He even wrote us a glowing letter upon his return to Dallas. It was dated August 25, 1988 and read:

"Dear Frank, thank you so much for the many courtesies extended to Weldon Aston, Bill Bogle and me while we were in Tampa earlier this week.

"You were very kind to arrange for the delightful dinner at the hotel. Our accommodations there were absolutely the finest, the food was marvelous, and even more important, our visit ended on the very positive note of accomplishing the results we had worked toward over these past weeks.

"I feel a great relief, and I am sure you do, too, that all the legal fine points have at last been handled, and we can move ahead to finalize our deal.

"Thanks again for everything. I look forward to seeing you again soon, and to working with you for a smooth, efficient transfer of ownership.

"Best personal regards,

"Sincerely, Eddie Chiles"

After so many years of frustration and near misses, we finally seemed to have broken through. Our agreement with Chiles, of course, didn't ensure that the deal was official yet. The proposed sale, which included the Rangers, the 43,508-seat Arlington Stadium and 119 acres of surrounding land, still had be approved by 10 of 14 American League owners and seven of 12 in the NL. In addition, there was the question of Dallas-based Gaylord Broadcasting, the minority owner of the franchise with 33 percent. Gaylord had 30 days first right of refusal on any sale and could conceivably try to buy the Rangers out from under us, keeping them right where they were.

We felt certain that wouldn't happen for two reasons. First, Edward Gaylord—the company's billionaire chairman who also owned superstations TNN and Fort Worth's KTVT, the Grand Ole Opry and The Daily Oklahoman newspaper—had attempted to purchase the Rangers in 1986 but was rejected by owners.

They weren't keen on the idea of allowing another owner with television superstations into baseball. Ueberroth had identified these cable giants as a problem for the game, because their vast signals could be picked up in every big-league market—as was the case with the Cubs on WGN, the Atlanta Braves with TBS and the New York Mets on WOR. Second, I had personally met with Gaylord president Glenn Stinchcomb and he assured me that Gaylord was a seller, not a buyer, in this deal.

But when news of the sale was trumpeted in headlines all over Dallas and Tampa Bay, Ed Gaylord suddenly became coy. He repeated in interviews that he wanted to take time to look at the details of the proposal before making a decision. Meanwhile, perhaps Chiles was beginning to feel the heat of local criticism for selling the Rangers to us. Word started to trickle out that perhaps he was frail and ill and wasn't in a proper frame of mind to make such a deal. He went on record in the press as saying he believed Gaylord would indeed try to exercise his option to buy the Rangers and keep them in Texas, and hoped he would.

An air of uncertainty had settled in. And without our knowledge, some shady business began to unfold in the background. Somebody, somewhere in baseball's power structure, decided they just didn't want us to have the team. Maybe it was more than one person. All we knew was that American League President Bobby Brown, a native of Texas, was in his home state scouting around for potential ownership. Remember this: Baseball always emphasized that a purchasing group had to have local ownership. We had 100 percent local ownership. But behind our back, Ueberroth and his team worked to assemble a team. A Washington Post story from 1999 recounts the background: "Anxious to get the franchise sold before he completed his tenure as commissioner in March 1989, Ueberroth and American League president Bobby Brown approached

Richard Rainwater, a prominent Forth Worth financier, and asked him to buy the team."

Rainwater, according to the Post story, invited a Dallas financier named Edward "Rusty" Rose III to join him for a meeting about becoming owners, but both men decided against it until Ueberroth asked that they talk to a well-known, well-connected individual related to a prominent political family in the United States: George W. Bush, the son of the Vice President and soon-to-be President, George H.W. Bush. "Ueberroth suggested they meet with Bush, who was eager to run the franchise," the story continued. "Within days, the seeds of the partnership were formed."

George W. was an old family friend of Eddie Chiles, so that reinforced the local connection even further. Fast forward a few weeks to the owners' two-day fall meeting in Montreal, where Bart Giamatti was set to be elected as Ueberroth's successor. Chiles was present and now publicly expressing regret for having sold the team to us.

"I'd feel a lot better and sleep a lot better if I hadn't made the deal, but a deal is a deal," he told reporters as the meetings got underway. "Human beings make mistakes and I confess I made a bad one. I wish I could correct it, but it turned around and bit me."

Both Ueberroth and Brown insisted that Chiles had nothing to worry about; the team wasn't going anywhere. And the next day, their statement became reality. Gaylord Broadcasting had decided to exercise its option and buy the Rangers— in spite of what I'd been told to my face. Just like that, the deal was undone. A *Chicago Tribune* story about the meetings said that if Gaylord hadn't stepped forward to buy the team, AL owners would have vetoed us. An unnamed NL owner was quoted in the story saying, "Gaylord is the lesser of two evils, but we don't want Gaylord, either. We don't want any more clubs owned by broadcast entities. We're going to do our best to find Eddie Chiles another buyer."

He was right on the money. Baseball owners then turned around and rejected Gaylord again, selling the Rangers instead to the group featuring George W. Bush, Rainwater, Rose and 39 investors in all. To label this a bitter pill would be a major understatement. For the life of me, I couldn't figure out why baseball had turned its back on us. We'd done everything they asked of us and played by their rules. And once again, the race had ended with us as nothing more than a stalking horse— helping baseball get what it wanted in the existing market.

I remembered once seeing the very last line in Ueberroth's 56-page contract as commissioner: The Commissioner can do whatever is in the best interest of baseball. Those words gave him total authority to do what he wanted, including circumventing our signed contract, if he thought he was acting in the best interest of the game. I admit that the thought of suing Major League Baseball crossed my mind, but I knew that would completely undermine any remaining chances we had.

We still believed our shot for a National League expansion team was excellent, especially given the strength of our group and how we'd worked with baseball all along. We returned home to Tampa discouraged but not defeated, feeling that baseball leaders would ultimately reward us for diligence. We turned our attention to expansion, and I signed a letter of intent with St. Petersburg Mayor Ulrich to put a team in the Suncoast Dome. We celebrated the moment in a special signing at home plate of Al Lang Stadium prior to a St. Louis Cardinals-Toronto Blue Jays spring training game. The lingering feud between Tampa and St. Petersburg had given way to a spirit of cooperation, born of necessity.

Not long after, new commissioner Giamatti announced that the National League would be announcing two new teams in 1991, ready to begin play in 1993. Many reports indicated that

Denver and Tampa-St. Petersburg were the two likely choices, though groups from Orlando, Miami and Phoenix were nudging into the picture. By now, I had spent more than $3 million of my own money during my eight-year pursuit of a baseball team and was facing serious financial difficulties with several banks that had loaned me money. Bill Mack, who had given us our financial clout from the start, had decided to reduce his role, which certainly didn't help our standing. But I regrouped with the addition of Central Florida businessmen Mark Bostick and Lance Ringhaver, and we felt good about our chances, given the long and winding road we'd followed so doggedly.

Then, on Dec. 19, 1990, I was on the Cheval golf course in Tampa at a Toys for Tots Christmas tournament. Someone brought me a fax from National League President Bill White. I read it hurriedly.

"Dear Mr. Morsani: Late this afternoon, the National League Executive Committee will have a press release announcing the 'short list' for expansion. There are six prospective ownership groups in six cities. I regret to inform you that your group is not on that list. ..." My heart sank. I was shocked, absolutely stunned. Even with all the other setbacks we'd experienced, this one stung the most. I left the course before reporters arrived, driving around aimlessly and trying to gather my thoughts. We were the only group that had met all the criteria. We had gone beyond what baseball leaders had asked of us, yet they still took advantage of us.

I'd always assumed that our fallback would be expansion, yet we hadn't even made the NL short list—losing out to a newly formed ownership group representing Tampa Bay. It consisted of a contingent headed by S. Joel Schur, co-owner of the Class A St. Petersburg Cardinals, and also included Sidney Kohl, a Milwaukee and Palm Beach resident who owned supermarkets and department stores in Wisconsin, Washington, D.C. lawyer Steven Porter and Roy Disney. Kohl and Disney packed the big bucks and Kohl was also a friend of Milwaukee Brewers owner and future commissioner Bud Selig.

They were the new torchbearers for a team for Tampa Bay, but it was a short-lived experience. On June 1, 1991, the National League awarded its two treasured expansion teams to Miami and Colorado—Tampa Bay had struck out once again.

Life was taking a particularly harsh turn. Even while being inducted in 1991 into the Tampa Bay Business Hall of Fame, I was dealing with a mounting problem with the banks. And I was mourning the loss of a wonderful man whose friendship I had come to cherish, our guide through the maze of baseball's mysterious and frustrating ways, Cedric Tallis. He died on May 8, 1991—living long enough to experience the personal hurt of being excluded from the final NL expansion cut. He passed away of a heart attack at age 76. But I honestly believe what killed him was a broken heart. He was just so upset that all our efforts didn't pan out. He'd been in major league baseball for more than 50 years and couldn't believe the people he worked with and respected would have acted in this way.

But there was no doubt in my mind now what I planned to do. I held off while Tampa businessman Vince Naimoli made his run at luring the San Francisco Giants to St. Petersburg in 1992, only to see his efforts derailed in such familiar fashion by baseball's power elite at the 11th hour. In this case, NL president White, a former Giant, worked behind the scenes on behalf of major league baseball to keep his old team in San Francisco rather than become the Tampa Bay Giants.

Naimoli, known for his feisty manner, filed a $3.5 billion lawsuit against baseball for its actions—a move that would ultimately lead owners to appease him by awarding him one of two AL expansion franchises in 1995, finally giving Tampa Bay a team that began play in the 1998 season.

Naimoli's suit certainly got the most attention around the game. But on Nov. 2, 1992—the day the Giants formally announced they were staying in San Francisco—I filed a lawsuit against Major League Baseball for $115 million on behalf of myself and members of the Tampa Bay Baseball Group. I wanted to wait until the Giants situation was fully resolved, to avoid interfering with Vince Naimoli and his group.

Our suit claimed that baseball acted in violation of Florida antitrust laws by illegally interfering with our attempt to buy the Twins and the Rangers, as well as our expansion efforts—resulting in Miami being awarded a franchise instead of Tampa Bay. Baseball succeeded in having the case moved to federal court, where it would have had an easier time. But our attorney, Tony Cunningham, prevailed in having the case returned to the Florida court system. That was a significant victory for us, and enjoying a baseball win for a change felt good.

But the road ahead was suddenly filled with a new and difficult challenge for Carol and me. Our only choice was to draw on reserves of strength we didn't know we had—and keep pushing toward a hint of daylight in the distance.

CHAPTER TEN

New Beginnings

As our search for a baseball team dragged on, the financial weight of the endeavor inevitably became a heavy strain on my monetary resources. Fortunately, my automobile companies were in good shape and never involved. But I'd had to borrow money from various banks to fund our major league mission. And in 1990, when the guaranteed notes on these loans came due, the banks had a legitimate question for me: How are we going to get paid back?

I hired a law firm to help me navigate through this new and formidable challenge. It's important to understand why we have a bankruptcy law in this country. In the early days of our history, England had debtors' prisons, but our Founding Fathers changed that practice and instead addressed the need for a uniform bankruptcy law in the U.S. Constitution. The first such act was passed in 1800, recognizing that some things happen in life because people make mistakes—or because of events that are beyond our control. In certain respects, that's what happened to us as a result of the unethical, unwarranted and completely unexpected treatment by Major League Baseball.

That said, the bankruptcy Carol and I eventually filed for in 1991 could have been avoided if not for one of four banks we were negotiating with. With the help of the law firm representing us—Stichter, Riedel, Blain and Prosser—we had arranged a deal that seemed workable. We owed money to the four banks,

and, with two of them, only a relatively small amount was involved—about $250,000. I had quite a few assets, including a
number of liquid assets—such as majority interest in a Savings
and Loan company in Ocala. The banks did their due diligence
and carefully pored over everything I had submitted. They
hired a certified public accounting firm run by Phil Piser, who
examined all of our earnings from my corporations and every
deal with a bank. He concluded that nothing I had ever done
showed any irregularities and everything I had given these
banks at any given point in time was accurately calculated and
recorded. In a nutshell, I was given a clean bill of health by an
independent source.

That step completed, we attended a meeting with the involved bankers to try to hammer out an acceptable agreement
for a payment plan. All the bankers in the room agreed that I
could pay them back at 60 cents on the dollar in cash. I had that
much cash and I could afford to do it, allowing me to avoid declaring bankruptcy. We scheduled another meeting for a week
later and I arrived expecting that the arrangement would be
approved. Our attorney, Richard Prosser, had prepared all the
documents for the officials to sign and everything was set to
go. But a representative of one of the banks, to which I owed
$150,000, began to quibble. His bank would have gotten 60
percent of the sum—and bear in mind, I write 60 percent off
on things all the time in my business. Much to my relief, the
official of that bank accepted the offer that day. But the next
morning we opened up the paper to see a headline that shook
us to the core: his bank was suing me.

Baseball had provided me with an entire lifetime's worth
of deals that had been jettisoned after an agreement had been
reached, but now it was happening again in my personal finances. Carol and I felt a torrent of emotions. We were furious,
bewildered, embarrassed. Because I didn't have enough money
to cover the debt, we had no choice but to declare Chapter

11. Now here's how a bankruptcy works with multiple lenders involved: They all must agree, or one bank can force you into declaring bankruptcy if it chooses. According to the rules, I couldn't pay one bank off and not pay the others. So there we were—in financial checkmate. Having lived my life within the rules, and worked every day to run a professional operation, this turn of events was excruciating. The only consolation was that the objecting bank could have had its 60 cents on the dollar if it had accepted my proposal. But after it forced us into bankruptcy, it wound up only getting eight cents on the dollar, thanks to the skillful work of my attorneys.

Carol's recollection of the situation hits the nail on the head: "The whole system is humiliating. You have to fill out forms every month detailing the money you spent—every dime. I was ornery, because I was the one filling out the forms. I wasn't spending a lot of money, but I'd itemize every little household item—just to give them a shot. They provided us with a stamp, and I still have the red inkpad that came with it. You had to stamp everything with this bankruptcy bit, making it as uncomfortable as possible. If we were fly-by-night people, we would have deserved it. But we didn't deserve the way we were treated."

After being in the public eye for so many years through my work with the Chamber of Commerce, followed by my efforts to land a baseball team for Tampa, it hurt suddenly to be thrust into the spotlight in such a negative manner. One of the local TV stations flew over our Pasco County ranch in a helicopter and aired a "hard-hitting" story to the effect of "this man is in bankruptcy and look at the nice home he owns!" The local press wouldn't let up on its coverage, including some of the very same outlets that had showered me with praise for all the work I'd done on other fronts. Carol and I laid low, staying home as much as possible to avoid the media. And we did our best to keep things in perspective, though it wasn't always easy.

We kept to our usual routine of waking up at 5:30 a.m., having a cup or two of coffee together and talking over whatever was going on in our lives. We reminded each other that we knew how to run a good company; that we would get through this. Carol knew me well enough to believe in my resolve: "Like I've said before, Frank has always, always, always been confident in what he can do. He said all along, 'We're going to come out of this. Keep your spirits up.' " That was the message I reinforced not only to Carol but to myself as well—"Get up in the morning, comb your hair, wash your face and look in the mirror: We've never done any man wrong. I'm comfortable with that.' And I told Carol, "As long as you're comfortable with that, that's how we'll live our lives. We didn't do anything wrong. We have an issue. I created it. And now we're going to fix it. I have sound companies and we're going to make it all work."

In times like these, I can't overstate the importance of friends. You learn very quickly who your real ones are. The morning the story that we were being sued hit the paper, we got a call from a good friend in the construction business, Mike Urette. "I said, 'I appreciate you calling, Mike,' and he responded, 'I'm at your gate.' " He'd simply come to offer moral support. There were a handful of others, too, like George Gage, the president of GTE, fellow GTE executive Bill Starkey and developer Earl Ware. They held a dinner for us to show their appreciation for what we'd done and try to buoy our spirits. To our surprise and disappointment, some friends abandoned us. But what mattered were those who did not. Our employees stood by us—we didn't lose a single one. The general managers didn't leave. They stayed right there, running and managing good companies. We'll always be grateful to everyone who never left our side in that dark period.

The process of repaying the debt lasted about a year, and we had to shed a few dealerships to generate money. It helped that none of the automobile manufacturers insisted that we pay cash on delivery. Nothing changed with our businesses, because I paid all our bills on time. The only lingering issue in such a situation is that a bankruptcy stays on the books for seven years, and it would have been visible to anybody who looked up our credit in that timeframe. But that was never a problem for us because we got back on our feet quickly.

Gradually, the ordeal began to fade into the background and we started to refocus on the path ahead. By this time, other than our close friends and family, we didn't really have much of a relationship with anybody. And we didn't engage in any activities, besides continuing our long tradition of teaching Sunday school classes at the Methodist Church. Both of us began doing that in Fort Lauderdale and we both taught in New Jersey, then in Tampa. That gave us a great deal of joy and helped us keep moving forward.

The lawsuit I had initiated against Major League Baseball was still in the early stages of what would be a lengthy, roller-coaster ride through the court system. While that continued to require my energy and attention, I knew it was time to re-immerse myself in my car business and find new opportunities on the horizon. It didn't take long for one to find me. This time it came in the form of football.

Back in the early '70s, football at the University of Tampa was a popular commodity in town. The Tampa Bay Bucs hadn't come into existence, there was no other college ball in the vicinity and UT's gridiron team featured such future NFL stars as Freddie Solomon and John Matuszak. At the same time, the university was struggling academically and financially and the emphasis on football was weighing down the school's development. This was a growing matter of concern for those of us who passionately wanted the university to flourish. Consequently, on Feb. 12, 1975, the board of trustees voted to drop football immediately. Years later, a man who was UT athletic director at the time wrote a book and alluded to a wealthy businessman who forced the school to get rid of the sport. He was referring to me.

The problem was that the University of Tampa, a small private institution, desperately needed the funds being funneled away by football. Ultimately, I was the board member who encouraged the school president to drop the sport, because we simply couldn't afford it any longer—football was losing more than $250,000 a year, which was a lot in those days.

The move was difficult but it paid off. I remained actively involved with UT as it evolved into a top-notch university, but I also began to develop a relationship with the relatively new state-funded school in the area, the University of South Florida, which had opened its doors two decades earlier. The university had honored me in 1981 with its Distinguished Citizen Award and included me in its President's VIP Group in 1986. I was well aware of the school's steady progress as an institution of higher learning. Yet the one thing the University of South Florida lacked, as a large and growing university, was a football program. In 1991, the university's President, Frank Borkowski, convened a group to study the feasibility of football at USF and recruited me to join his 37-member committee. We concluded that football was not only feasible but desirable and recommended, on March 20, 1992, that the sport be added.

The USF Athletics Council took up the matter right away and began soliciting input from all corners of the campus. Then, on December 3, 1992, the council overwhelmingly passed a resolution—by a 15-2 vote—recommending that President Borkowski seek non-state resources to fund football at USF. For all intents and purposes, this was the starting point.

The job of raising money for this landmark effort fell to two individuals: Payton Adams, retired president of GTE Telephone Operations Southern Division, and me. On June 30, 1993, we were named co-chairs of a 14-member Fund Raising Steering Committee for USF Intercollegiate Football. The plan called for USF to field a Division 1-AA team for the 1997 season. To meet that somewhat ambitious deadline, we were charged with a $5 million endowment goal by the end of '93 and the job of raising a second $5 million within two years. The pressure to raise the initial $5 million arose from the need to assure approval from the Board of Regents to start at the 1-AA level. The second $5 million would pave the way for the school to reach the ultimate goal of Division 1-A status.

At the press conference to unveil the big news, I explained to the press my reasons for getting involved. "I think football is an important part of campus life, and it's something that a major urban institution like USF should have. I wouldn't get involved in something like this unless it was being done the right way. And this process is the right way. I do believe the resources are there. It certainly should be doable for us." We'd already gotten off to a great start with $3 million in pledges toward the program. Now it was time to get in gear for the rest, and I relished the chance to help the relatively young university take an important step in its evolution.

One month later, an important development occurred. USF named beloved former Tampa Bay Buccaneer star Lee Roy Selmon as Associate Athletic Director of External Affairs under athletic director Paul Griffin. There was no more respected athlete in the history of Tampa Bay area sports. Lee Roy had worked in the banking business after a back injury in 1985 led to his retirement from the NFL, and he and I were about to become a terrific tag-team in the art of raising money.

When Lee Roy came on board, I sat down with him and said, "You've been a winner all of your life. You've had all this adulation in high school, college ball at the University of Oklahoma and with the Bucs. You've never been a failure at any point in your life. Unfortunately, if you haven't had some failures, it's going to be difficult." Now I know that Lee Roy experienced failure in a team sense with the epic 0-26 start of the Bucs. My point was to stress the importance of learning and growing from personal setbacks. I was pleased to see how quickly he adjusted to the new challenge, and his name recognition proved invaluable as he and I set out to raise money for USF football.

We went all over the Tampa Bay area, speaking to anyone who might be in a position to contribute significantly to the program. Carol, who occasionally observed us in action, remembers how well we worked together: "They'd go out talking to various donors or corporations and Frank would say, 'Now before we go in there, we're going to ask for a certain amount of money. And Lee Roy would say, 'You can't do that! How do you know they can afford that?' He'd never gone out and asked anybody for money and didn't really know how to raise money at first. That was Frank's strong suit. They were funny together."

I understood his reaction to the challenge of asking for money on a grand scale, but told him, "Remember, Lee Roy, you don't want to insult somebody's wallet or pocketbook by not asking for enough.' If you ask for $50,000, you'll only get $10,000." We gave a lot of speeches together. I would start out talking, and then I'd introduce Lee Roy. Of course, he went to OU and I went to Oklahoma State. We had a good time going back and forth about that. I'd say to whatever group we were addressing, "Lee Roy couldn't get into a good school. He had to go to Oklahoma," and that would break the ice. One donor at a time, he and I raised a substantial amount of money for USF football. He could call anybody in town and get an audience. I always said to him, "Lee Roy, you can open the door—and I'll close." And that's how we would do it.

We easily met the first deadline for $5 million in December, 1993. That was the same month Betty Castor was named USF's president, after Frank Borkowski left to become chancellor at Appalachian State. Betty embraced the football effort and its potential for spurring widespread support for the school, both among students and alumni. A season ticket drive followed, resulting in 2,000 commitments by 1995—a year that began with Lee Roy becoming the first Buccaneer elected to the Pro Football Hall of Fame. And by June of '95, we had raised the additional $5 million to keep USF football on track. Now, it all came down to whether we would receive official approval from the Board of Regents.

It fell to me to address the Board and make final the case for finalizing the commitment to football. Despite all the money we'd raised—close to $12 million—members of the Board of Regents expressed a concern that while the money looked impressive in terms of pledges, it might not represent a firm financial commitment. As I listened to their worries, I leaned over in my seat and whispered to President Castor, "Betty, make a telephone call and see if you can find out how many people didn't make good on their pledges when the private sector in Tampa raised $32 million for the construction of the Tampa Bay Performing Arts Center." I knew that everyone had paid their pledges on that $32 million.

She got on the phone and found out that less than one-half of one percent hadn't paid. That type of follow-through is hard to achieve in pledge campaigns anywhere, yet typical of the support I had seen on charitable initiatives in this town.

When my time came to speak, I closed with that example. "In our community, everyone pays their debt."

"Now that we have raised the money," I continued, "when you bless this endeavor, I am confident that the community's support will be overwhelming."

The Board voted to approve, officially giving life to football at USF on September 15, 1995. One day later, the university began its search for the program's first head coach, hiring Jim Leavitt on December 3, 1995—and celebrating its first-ever game with an 80-3 win over Kentucky Wesleyan at Tampa Stadium on September 6, 1997. What a tremendous feeling of accomplishment we all enjoyed that day.

Another key date in the progression of USF sports came in March 2001. Athletic Director Paul Griffin had become embroiled in a controversy over allegations of racial discrimination involving African-American members of the women's basketball team. President Judy Genshaft had just arrived at the school during the previous summer and found herself in the midst of a highly charged atmosphere.

The situation grew progressively ugly, lasting for some four months before reaching a crisis. In an effort to find a solution, President Genshaft brought in a Florida Supreme Court judge who was African-American to help as a consultant. In the end, she asked athletic director Griffin to step down from a post he'd held for 15 years.

The search for a new athletic director began right away, leading to Lee Roy Selmon. I'm honored by Judy Genshaft's recollection of my input in the process: "I worked with Frank—he was very thoughtful and very good in providing advice. He met with Lee Roy and was gentle but forthright in telling him how hard the job would be in managing and leading people. Lee Roy said, 'Well, I think I'm ready.' I believed he was, too, and hired him. Lee Roy was a community icon, and immediately had a calming, unifying effect as our new athletic director."

In that capacity, he was the man who oversaw the growth of the football program, with the university's move into Conference USA and eventually the Big East. When health reasons prompted Lee Roy to resign after three years on the job in 2004, he continued to have an impact in his new role as president of the USF Foundation Partnership for Athletics. We both savored the construction and completion of the Frank Morsani Football Practice Complex in February 2011, a project to which I contributed $3 million—with its two full-sized fields of Bermuda grass and one regulation artificial turf field.

It still seems hard to believe that, only eight months later, he was gone. The warm, decent giant of a man suffered a massive stroke on September 2, 2011 and died shortly after at only 56 years of age. The world lost a wonderful person that day. And I lost a friend.

I've accumulated many keepsakes over my life. But one that I am particularly fond of is a glossy photo of Lee Roy and me grinning at one another at a 1995 press conference—thrilled at the big news that USF would have a football program. The picture is inscribed with a black Sharpie, sporting a simple message.

"Frank, we started in 1993. Thanks to you, football at USF is a reality in 1995. Go Bulls.

"Lee Roy Selmon."

CHAPTER ELEVEN

Building Dreams

We didn't start out with a grand plan to enrich the places that had touched our lives and the lives of so many others. The process evolved gradually, in stages, all from being part of a city that had given us a foundation and a good home. We came to look at charitable giving as our responsibility—a way to create a better quality of life and more opportunities in our community, whether in education, the arts, health care or athletics. This became the final phase in the guiding philosophy that had shaped our journey—the cycle of learn, earn and return. We had come from humble roots and worked hard in school to open new doors, worked hard to create financial advantages, and now found ourselves moving through the 1990s and beyond motivated by a deeply held desire to invest what we had amassed along the way.

As I mentioned, the first substantial gift we gave was spurred by a personal connection to one of my employees who had died from cancer. When ground was broken for the construction of the Moffitt Cancer Center in 1983, we decided to give money to help the hospital help others. We donated a room and funded a chair, totaling several million dollars at that time. It became the start of a special relationship for us that would grow stronger and more meaningful through the years ahead. Of course, the bond we soon began to cement with the University of South Florida defined our philanthropic direction as much as anything—and continues to do so in many edifying ways to this day.

I had been so heavily involved in the University of Tampa in the 1970s that USF was hardly on my radar. That began to change when Carol and I met a man named Carl Riggs, the Vice President of Academic Affairs at the University of South Florida. Our paths crossed in a group we'd joined on campus called "The Cadre," dedicated to supporting and savoring the arts at USF. It turned out that Carl had graduated from the University of Oklahoma, so we had a natural bond through our Okie roots.

I recall Carl asking why I'd gravitated so much to UT and I explained that it was a smaller, private university that needed assistance, as opposed to a large school financed by the government such as USF. But he educated me about public universities, particularly how funding was declining at that time. He explained that while 50-to-60 percent came from the state, the remainder hinged on grants or student fees. (As a side note, state funding today is less than 25 percent!) Consequently, there was a serious need for private assistance to fill the void. I talked to Carol and we decided that perhaps we should divide our efforts and help both schools. That's how we got involved at USF. At first, it took the form of lectures at the business school, giving talks on entrepreneurship. We didn't give any substantial money at this point, but we started to get to know the university better and our sense of connection slowly took root.

The next pivotal step came in tandem with another friend, Tampa businessman Rudy Michaud, who had brought Metropolitan Life Insurance Company to Tampa. I'd gotten to know Rudy through my involvement with the Tampa Chamber of Commerce and one day he asked if I would serve as co-chair of the University of South Florida's first capital campaign. Rudy is a wonderful man and I liked the idea of teaming up with him on such a worthwhile endeavor. I'm proud to say that we wound up raising $117 million by the time the capital campaign ended its roughly five-year mission in 1991. That allowed the university to make important new strides and set the stage for the landmark push to bring football to USF.

But our efforts and financial commitments weren't entirely aimed at the university. Our friendship with fellow Oklahoman Carl Riggs led us to re-establish a connection with our alma mater, Oklahoma State, during the mid-1980s. I gave the commencement speech at OSU in 1986 and, in time, we would start making donations to invest in the school that had provided each of us with such an excellent education—not to mention the place Carol and I reconnected. We gave the school substantial money for scholarships and a program in ethics, and contributed to the building of a dormitory.

Yet the more we donated, the more I felt it was important to encourage others with financial means to do the same. So many worthy causes in a community depend on support from the private sector, but many people in a position to help choose not to—or don't give as much as they can afford to. That became the driving force on May 20, 1996 when Carol and I made a sizeable donation to a pair of local organizations so vital to the area. Let me emphasize that I feel uncomfortable talking here about the specific amount of our donations, even though they have been covered heavily in the local media and are part of the public record. My intention is not to shine the spotlight on us or seek praise in any way, but simply to let others with financial means know how their contributions can enrich the community in which they live and work.

That said, we gave $5 million to the nine-year-old Tampa Bay Performing Arts Center, to be put toward its $20 million endowment campaign. And we also contributed $3 million to the Community Foundation of Tampa Bay, with our intention that the money support such local charities as the Spring,

Hospice, the Home Association and music education in public schools.

I'll never forget the beautiful ceremony at the Performing Arts Center, overlooking the Hillsborough River, when Carol and I made the official announcement. "We adopted Tampa 25 years ago and have been overwhelmed by kindness and openness in this community," I told the audience. "We want our gift to be a token of our gratitude and love for the Tampa Bay area." But I also wanted to explain why Carol and I felt it was important to attach our names to the gift, one described as the largest single philanthropic donation in Tampa at the time. We didn't do it out of a desire for acclaim or attention—far from it. In a period of budgetary woes for non-profit organizations, we wanted our names to serve as a wake-up call to others in a position to lend a hand.

Our intention was to make a statement, to hopefully inspire other potential donors throughout the Tampa Bay area. Our late friend Jim Shimberg, whose theater producer brother Hinks Shimberg had brought Broadway to Tampa Bay, sat on the board of trustees of both the TBPAC and the Community Foundation. Jim described the donation as the largest either organization had received. He told media covering the event, "The greatest significance of this gift is the example it sets for other people in our community."

We structured the gift in a way that it could keep giving. Carol and I actually donated $5 million to the permanent endowment fund of the Community Foundation. Income generated from that would provide the Tampa Bay Performing Arts Center with a permanent source of revenue for programming and upkeep. And the $3 million was placed in a charitable remainder trust, with income that it creates helping the Foundation support its many charities.

It was hard not to get teary-eyed as I spoke—I'm a crier as my family and friends well know, and this was one of those occasions. I choked up feeling keenly aware of how people who deserved this opportunity would enjoy a new place for artistic expression.

"If we are in an era of less government intrusion in our lives, we citizens have to step up to the pump," I told the gathering. "We have to step up and be counted."

"It is our hope that this gift will encourage others to be generous to the many nonprofit organizations in our community, which are so vital to enriching mankind."

Carol also spoke to the media, adding, "Through the arts we learn to appreciate beauty, which in turn enriches the lives of children and adults."

Ultimately, we selected the TBPAC because we viewed it as a centerpiece of culture in the Tampa Bay Area, a showcase for celebrating achievement in the arts. And we were delighted that the Center's Executive Director, Judy Lisi, saw the gift as a way of providing important support for performing artists throughout Tampa Bay. I had come to know Judy as a good friend from the first day we met. I had decided to stop by the Performing Arts Center to offer assistance soon after she started in 1992. She tells the story of that first meeting like this:

"It was my first month on the job and somebody knocked on my door. And here was this very nice man who said, 'Hello, my name is Frank Morsani and I have a check for your center for $15,000.' I can tell you it was a fantastic way to meet somebody!"

For me, and for Carol, that day marked the start of a highly meaningful association with Judy and the center. The same year that we made our $5 million donation, I had another surprise announcement—and this time Carol knew nothing about it ahead of time. I arranged to have the showcase 2,600-seat theater within the center, Festival Hall, renamed Carol Morsani Hall. Carol acknowledges that she never saw it coming: "He did that all on his own—I didn't even know it was in the works until it was a done deal."

I've been blessed with a wonderful woman who has tolerated me through the years and I wanted to find a fitting way to honor her. It can be a rough road for a wife when you do all the things I've done in my career, constantly working and moving. She never complained. For that reason, it was an absolute pleasure spending the $5 million to fund a Performing Arts Center endowment and to place Carol's name on the hall. In addition, my feeling was that personalizing the identity of the hall with Carol's name would serve as an impetus for others to donate money to the center or for naming rights to its other performance halls.

When it comes to the arts, the importance of making such a move in the form of an endowment—something in which I believe strongly—is particularly important in the state of Florida. You can't depend upon the government to support anything in Florida for one basic reason: The state is now home to 20-million people — the third largest state in the country — and our infrastructure problems are enormous. Florida does not have the capacity to support culture, and it is imperative for donors to take up the slack caused by insufficient governmental assistance.

Carol tried to talk me out of naming the hall strictly for her, suggesting we broaden it to include the Morsani Family. That was not surprising, given her modest, down-to-earth nature. "I'm basically shy and I didn't want the attention. I was fearful that my life would change and thought people would stop me and say, 'Hey, aren't you the woman whose name is on the building?' Well, it turns out that many people don't even associate it with me anyway." Two years after the name change, I began what would become a nine-year run as chairman of the board of the Performing Arts Center, ending in 2007. Today,

I feel immense pride that the venue has never been in better shape physically or financially.

I've teamed with Hinks Shimberg, whose aforementioned Broadway bookings have helped the Center's revenues immeasurably. Together, we raised $65 million toward our goal of a $100 million endowment. Others have stepped up with significant contributions through naming rights—the Shimberg Playhouse, honoring Hinks and his wife, Elaine; the Patel Conservatory for arts education; Louise Lykes Ferguson Hall; the TECO Energy Foundation Theater; and David A. Straz Jr.'s landmark contribution, resulting in the change from the Tampa Bay Performing Arts Center to the Straz Center.

Judy Lisi's assessment of Carol and me and the work we set out to do means a tremendous amount. "He hoped others would follow his lead, and it worked. This area wouldn't be the place it is without Frank and Carol—if you look at what they've done for us, for the universities, for Moffitt. People with resources are very good at attaining wealth, but then they have to be reminded what to do with it. And I think Frank has really set the tone for what you need to do. It's hard to know what would have happened if he hadn't set the bar so high."

It's very satisfying to know we could help in all those important components of a community. If you look at where we were with philanthropy over the past few decades in Tampa Bay, special mention should be made of the three people who have made a point of giving significantly in Pinellas County: my friend Tom James, Chairman of the Board of Raymond James Financial; William Hough, founder of William R. Hough and Company investment firm; and the late Jack Eckerd. Jack endowed the Eckerd Family Foundation with $100 million from his chain of drug stores—and Ruth Eckerd Hall, named for his wife, has proven to be a tremendous addition to the cultural scene.

I recall a special gathering of high-powered individuals from Pinellas County that Tom convened to raise money for the Salvador Dali Museum on the St. Petersburg waterfront. He'd asked me to serve on the museum board and I was glad to oblige and help anyway I could. When the fundraising event started, Tom got the ball rolling with a pledge of $1 million and remarked, "Who else will give?" There was an uncomfortable silence. So I jumped in with a pledge of $500,000. When nobody followed suit, I said with a smile, 'Wait, I'm from Tampa and I'm kicking in a half-million dollars!" That seemed to break the ice, and others in the room stepped up. I'm grateful for Tom's kind words about my role with Dali: "Frank donated his business management and leadership skills as well as assisted financially. Moreover, he demonstrated great interpersonal skill and was a pleasure to worth with in the process."

As far as Carol and I are concerned, our theory has always been, if you'll give, then other people will come on board. And they have. That has always been the reason we've done these things, trying to lead the charge and leave the world a better place. That is our objective in life, whether through leadership or through financial support. It's not for accolades or hash marks on our sleeves, and we are so pleased to see the reality of increased involvement on the community landscape.

Our own personal landscape continued to be enormously fulfilling through the 1990s and into the new century. My automotive business thrived, at one point including 30 dealerships around the country. Our hard work was honored with the Sports Illustrated All-Star Dealer Award in 1995—15 years after the magazine awarded us with the Import Automobile Dealer Distinction Award. That same year, at age 63, I considered a run for the U.S. House of Representatives, which would have put me up against my old friend, 17-term Democratic Congressman Sam Gibbons.

I'd always backed Sam before, but my feeling was it was important to reduce the scope of the federal government while shifting programs back to the state, "I'm not anti-government— I'm anti-poor government," I stated at the time. In the end, I decided against running, partly because I was unable to pin down then-Florida state senator Charlie Crist on whether he'd run. I didn't want to get into a protracted campaign against Crist in case he chose to throw his hat in the ring. Instead, he stayed on the sidelines, Sam announced he was retiring and Mark Sharpe emerged as the Republican candidate. He eventually lost to the candidate Sam endorsed, Jim Davis, who rode President Bill Clinton's coattails to a resounding 15-point win.

Another win during this time period closed the door on a bitter chapter in our lives. On Sept. 26, 2003, after 11 years of litigation, the suit I filed along with 14 other former members of the Tampa Bay Baseball Group was finally settled with Major League Baseball. The settlement was reached when the involved parties agreed to hire a mediator, leading to a resolution one month before the case was finally to go to trial in Tampa. We had the facts on our side and we never gave up hope that justice would prevail—even with frustrating delays, seven different judges, two moves to federal court, and two subsequent appeals to Florida's Supreme Court, resulting in an outcome that at last we could live with.

By the rules of the settlement, I can't disclose the terms. But our dogged attorney, Tony Cunningham, put it in perspective when he told the media, "It was amicably settled by all parties. We're happy to finish a major piece of litigation." The reality is, the banks got most of the money out of that deal. But needless to say, it felt good to be validated by the court system after having endured so many headaches and heartaches at the hands of baseball—when all we ever did was play within the rules they gave us. Besides that affirmation by the courts, Carol reminds me that I did get one other thing in the aftermath. "He bought himself a new car."

Neither Carol nor I allowed the lawsuit to be a distraction during those years, though it easily could have been with all its frustrating twists and turns. Carol immersed herself in many projects that contributed meaningfully to the community. As an interior design student in college, she was drawn to art and, in the late 1970s and early 1980s, served on the Board of the Tampa Museum of Art. She was on the building committee that oversaw the construction of the stunning new museum in nearby Curtis Hixon Park downtown. Carol also has remained active through the years on the foundation board of Moffitt Cancer Center, to which we have donated several million dollars and additional money to fund a handful of endowed chairs. We'll give them another sum upon our deaths.

The important aspect of the gifts is that Moffitt benefits now from the interest generated from the money we gave, without having to draw from the principal. Adds Carol: "The Chairs are to support the people doing such critical research. We always have wanted the money to go toward a better understanding of cancer and working toward cures, rather than bricks and mortar. Both sides of our family have been affected by cancer so this is an area where we've wanted to help."

Beyond her involvement in the museum and Moffitt, Carol has been on the board of the Florida Orchestra. She has led USF Women in Leadership & Philanthropy, a group whose mission is to empower female students and faculty. She served as president of a fund-raising arm of the American Heart Association, the Hearts of Gold. Carol has one herself, and I was proud when the Tampa Chamber of Commerce named her Cultural Contributor of the Year in 2002.

Our work together under the umbrella of the Frank and Carol Morsani Foundation has given both of us a great deal of joy. We've looked for ways to make a difference for people and places that are making a difference, such as the university that helped forge our direction early on, Oklahoma State. In 2007, we were excited and honored to pledge a large gift from our estate to OSU's College of Education. That established the Frank Morsani Distinguished Chair in Education, held by the Dean of the College of Education, as well as the Frank Morsani Distinguished Chair of Excellence in Ethical Leadership. And the centerpiece of the gift brings us tremendous gratification: the Frank and Carol Morsani Center for Ethics and Creative Leadership.

We were also pleased to give money to endow chairs in mathematics and science, two areas where we need to continue to make strides in today's world. While we don't do this for personal recognition, we feel highly appreciative of the honors bestowed on us in return—such as the Henry G. Bennett Award, OSU's highest humanitarian award, in 2005; the naming of Morsani Hall, a student dorm at Oklahoma State; the College of Education's annual award for staff excellence; and a special moment in 2010 when Carol and I were each presented with honorary Doctor of Letters degrees from the university. It was particularly special in light of the infrequency that Oklahoma State bestows the honor. Dating back to its founding in 1890—17 years before Oklahoma was granted statehood — only 16 individuals had received honorary doctorates. We were numbers 17 and 18.

We've developed a wonderful friendship with Oklahoma State President Burns Hargis and we deeply appreciate his words about us:

"I was well aware of their success in business and their impact in philanthropy when I met them, but I think what took me aback is how enthusiastic they are about life. There's just an unquenchable zest that they have for life, which keeps them young. They come from humble beginnings yet they are humble themselves. When I first visited them in Tampa, we drove through downtown and passed Carol Morsani Hall—and neither of them said anything. I looked up and said, 'Hey, your name is on the building.' And they just said, 'Oh yeah, we try to help out.' All I can say is the breadth of their philanthropy and involvement is remarkable."

It's certainly no secret that we feel a unique sense of involvement with and a passion for a school we never attended, the University of South Florida. Though our relationship began almost by chance, our desire grew steadily stronger to help this young state institution become a powerful, nationally regarded center of learning. It tapped in me that innate desire to figure out ways to make things work. And now, at this stage of life, I was in a position to help others do that by offering financial assistance. Following my involvement in the first capital campaign and the creation of football, the next key step came when we chaired the second capital campaign from 1996-2001. We raised more than $255 million, earmarked for a wide range of academic programs and expansion projects.

Carol and I never expected anything in return for the work. But it would be less than truthful to say we weren't sincerely moved when we each received honorary Doctor of Letters degrees from the University of South Florida in 2005. The school went out of its way to give us our own individual presentations. I'm so glad, because Carol most certainly deserved her own recognition—even if it made her uncomfortable to be in the spotlight of such praise from President Genshaft: "Mrs. Morsani has been described as a remarkable leader who can invoke selflessness and passion in those she encounters." I had to agree. And Judy's closing words made me tear up.

"Both Carol and Frank Morsani share a passion for higher education. Their support for USF to become a top-tier institution is contagious and their tireless enthusiasm and generosity is commendable. They both have brought honor to the

University of South Florida through their achievements and humanitarian contributions."

It was during this period that the university undertook an ambitious plan for a state-of-the-art health care facility on campus, estimated to cost $64 million. The Dean of the Medical School, Dr. Steven Klasko, came to us and laid out his vision—essentially a "one-stop-shopping" clinic that would house physicians, nurses and medical students in one clinic with 60 outpatient exam rooms and cutting-edge diagnostic equipment to dramatically accelerate the entire evaluation process. He saw a medical setting in which a patient could get treatment and diagnosis in a matter of hours—instead of spending days or weeks to get care, with the burden of multiple appointments and travel. The over-arching idea was to create a model for a new kind of efficient, attentive health care delivery nationwide—and for preparing medical students to become the doctors of tomorrow. Steve saw this clinic as a way to fundamentally change medical care in the future.

We loved the idea and wanted to help. That ultimately led us to a watershed moment in our commitment to USF. On June 1, 2006, Carol and I gave the university a gift of $10 million—$7-million of which was designated for the clinic and an additional $3-million to go to a new football practice complex and a new stadium for the women's softball team. The scene at the press conference to announce the news was memorable—a standing-room-only crowd of medical students, school administrators, football and softball players and cheerleaders. We even got a big hug from Rocky the Bull, the USF mascot. And, once again, we were touched by the comments from President Genshaft: "This is a leadership gift. It will immeasurably transform two major projects at USF. The Morsanis understand the critical role of vision in building our community and our university."

Truthfully, we couldn't have been more thrilled to make this contribution, both for those in the medical field dedicated to making an impact in advanced patient health care and for the dreams of so many USF athletes. More funds would certainly be needed for the 194,000-square-foot health building, but we hoped our gift would spur those donations to cover the overall price tag. We were immensely humbled when the Carol and Frank Morsani Center for Advanced Health Care opened in 2008. Yet our interest in helping further invest in health care at USF—and beyond—soon would lead us down a new road.

Working again with Steven Klasko, we saw the need to rebuild the medical school's four-decades-old facilities—a challenge that would require state and private funding. As usual, we felt we could lead the way on the private side, and our decision was made with the deepest belief in USF's ability to blaze a new path in health care. Our gift in December 2011 of $20 million—raising our overall commitment to the university to $43 million—would serve as a catalyst in the campaign to raise the needed $60 million. The gift resulted in the USF medical school being renamed the Morsani College of Medicine, and at the ensuing press conference I once again underscored the philosophy Carol and I share: "We're not Donald Trump or those people that want their name on something. That's never been why we have given a nickel to anything. We hope this encourages others to say, 'Let's examine what we are going to do with our resources.' "

We feel good that our resources have set in motion plans for the creation of a breathtakingly modern, open building—a place to promote easy collaboration among the university's various health care schools and keep USF at the forefront of the ever-changing medical landscape in this country. In addition, a portion of our donation has opened the door for the Klasko

Institute for an Optimistic Future in Healthcare, designed to nurture creative solutions and strategies in medicine.

All our support of USF, particularly in health care, doesn't mean Carol and I have turned our backs on the first area school I enjoyed working with—the University of Tampa. UT is a treasure, and has become one of the nation's fine private universities. We were glad to make a multi-million-dollar estate gift in 2013 to the school, resulting in the naming of an existing residential hall and student center as Frank and Carol Morsani Hall. The contribution mirrored our feeling that Tampa Bay is a far better place due to the academic excellence of the University of Tampa—and that our commitment to education isn't limited to one school over another, as Judy Genshaft has so graciously noted:

"Many university presidents would get very jealous if you gave a large sum of money to another school, but Frank says, 'Look, I'm a graduate of Oklahoma State. I like my president there and I give to the school. When he gave money to the University of Tampa, I wrote him a note of congratulations—thank you for helping the Tampa Bay community. Because that is who he is. When people give, they have enough for everybody. Frank and Carol are all about giving to good causes and not getting into the politics of it. They are the premier role models. They are giving without strings attached, giving for the cause of helping others. They enjoy doing that—and certainly we are grateful.

"In so many ways, Frank's generosity has brought the university to a whole new level. But it's not just through generosity. He participates in search committees. If you call him and ask whether he would want to serve on the Alzheimer's board, he'll go, 'Yeah, I'd love to do that.' He gives talks to classrooms and to our administrators. He's an outstanding speaker, who rarely needs notes. The students love him, because he has so much to offer.

"And he not only gives money, but he gets money for us. He's very active as a fundraiser. He also wants us to have more of a national profile, so he'll use his own money to create sponsorships of events designed to get us that national attention."

I have to return the kind words to Judy. She's a tremendously smart woman and an excellent administrator. And both Carol and I are very fond of her. She's not afraid of making decisions and she's been very supportive of what we've done. I should add that not everything we've undertaken at the university has required heavy lifting. One of our great pleasures in recent years was to serve on a panel of judges for a talent show among USF medical students, a charity fundraiser called BAN-Daids for Bridge. You would absolutely not have believed the level of talent displayed by these fine young men and women—dancing, singing, playing classical instruments like virtuosos.

It was hard not to get misty-eyed, thinking about these kids and how hard they are working to contribute to society. These are medical students and yet they still had time for this. Maybe my emotions were tied to learning the rigors of hard work from a childhood many years ago on the farms of Arkansas and Oklahoma, growing up with parents and grandparents who created opportunities for their family through personal sacrifice.

It was a life that forever instilled in me the love of hard work, and a feeling of renewed hope when I see young people doing what it takes to build their own dreams. People often talk about how the kids of today are taking the easy road or don't apply themselves enough. That's just not true. Many of the students on campus work one or two jobs to put themselves through school. When you are with them, you know there are many wonderful young people out there, on a course to do wonderful things. Perhaps seeing that helps keep Carol and me stay young at heart.

We have been blessed to walk our path together for all these years, doing what we can to make our community a better place. And the biggest gift for us comes from lighting the path for those who go where the work is, enriching life today and shaping the world tomorrow.

The Essence of Entrepreneurialism

Most people don't know that I once was in the perfume business. That may sound surprising, given all the time I devoted to so many other pursuits. But at the time, perfume seemed like a good investment and I gave it my best shot. I should say "we"—given that the idea for the venture came from a colleague in the car business.

This fellow, Patrick, had dreamed up a plan to create and market perfume and approached me about it back in the 1980s. You might think that I'd have done a double-take when a topic like that was broached out of the blue. But I heard him out and was intrigued, responding, "Let's see if we can do that." Patrick was from France—the President of Peugeot USA—and a very bright man. I got to know him when we bought him out, but I didn't expect to get a side business out of the deal, too.

We began to study perfume, learning that the basis of it was—of all things—the residue of cognac. My new partner then traveled to the famed Hennessy cognac distillery in Cognac, France along the Rue de Crouin, where we obtained all of our perfume byproduct. The best part of the deal was that the byproduct we needed was free because the Hennessy people were just throwing away so much of that cognac residue. Once we had enough to work with, we enlisted experienced help to

create the actual perfume. And I have to say that it had a terrific fragrance—it even got Carol's thumbs up.

Our next step was to decide how to market the product
amid so many available established brands. We came up with
the idea of selling to boutiques, which could customize the
perfume using their own packaging and store names. We made
a list of all the local beauty shops and approached them with
samples—and many of them loved it. They especially liked the
idea of being able to sell perfume to customers with their store
label imprinted on it. We created special packaging for every
outlet, and wound up producing this new perfume in small
shops and department stores throughout the Tampa Bay region. We had a successful perfume run for several years until
Patrick went back into the car business and sold his share to
another man. That's when I decided to end my short but rewarding career in the fragrance industry.

I bring this story up for a reason, which has less to do with
perfume than it does with smelling a business opportunity
when one arises. Over the years, I've actually started a number
of businesses; some are extensions of my primary occupation
with automotive dealerships; others have no connection. You
might be surprised by the variety.

They have included: a leasing company; an insurance undertaking called Freedom Credit Life and Accidental Death; a
property and casualty company; a small business investment
operation; a place that made the paper that goes on billboards,
with offices in Tampa, Miami, Jacksonville and Pensacola; an
850-acre cattle ranch in Pasco County; a construction business named Canco General Contractors, which I bought when
the out-of-state owner became ill; an advertising company; an
investment firm—and even a trading company in Hangzhou,

China. Because of my success in the import car business, I decided I'd like to give the import-export business a try.

Building on contacts from my experience in Hangzhou, I opened a business that imported rubber from Malaysia to manufacture 100 percent rubber gloves used by doctors and nurses, and then sold those gloves to medical personnel and hospitals in the United States. In addition, we bought tires from Korea and sold them to businesses in South America—accepting payment in the form of imported lumber, which we proceeded to sell at home. That's how we made a profit. But that all came to an abrupt end with the Tiananmen Square Massacre in June 1989, when the Chinese military smashed the pro-democracy movement in the country. Thousands of demonstrators were killed in the violence, and my trading company was obliterated in the process.

Over the years, I've known a number of people who have wanted to invest or open businesses in China. My own experience has taught me a lesson, and I'm glad to impart it to others: If you plan to start a business in any developing country, I advise against putting your own money into the enterprise. Instead, borrow the funds from a bank—such as the Bank of China. With that strategy, you are assured that your business will be safe, since the bank will want to get back the money it has invested. I did not follow that business practice in my dealings with the Hangzhou trading company, and I paid a price— but I've learned from my failures as well as my successes. In this instance, I learned the importance of not only knowing the laws of every state in which you do business, but every country as well.

In time, I sold off most of my companies to my employees, a practice I've always liked to follow. But you might wonder why did I start all these companies in the first place? The answer is simple: there was an opportunity, a niche, a chance to offer something that would be of value to people in the marketplace.

I'd think, "Well, I can do that. I've heard about this and I think it's worth taking a shot." Generally, the process begins when somebody comes to me with an idea, and I take time to evaluate the potential. Take, for example, a business venture with the former president of the University of Tampa, Bob Owens. He left Tampa to run a college in Missouri but when he retired, he moved back to town and talked to me about starting an insurance company together. That made sense to me; we had so many dealerships that were generating revenue for insurance companies, I figured we might as well do it for ourselves. The idea for a local small business investment company, meanwhile, came from my years serving on President Reagan's Small Business Advisory Council. I thought, "Maybe we can do that down here in Tampa." I assembled a group, attracted some investors and we started financing small businesses.

This gets to the heart of my belief in the importance of entrepreneurialism. In short, people can make a mark if they are alert to opportunities that arise, and know how to parlay those opportunities into products or services. That's why I have always enjoyed giving lectures about free enterprise and entrepreneurship to college students. I find they are very eager to hear about this—and, in truth, it's a fundamental part of who I am, stemming from my life-long desire to figure out how things work and how to fix them when they don't. I look at opportunities the same way—will a business work, what will make it run best, and how can I get it on course if it needs help?

As you can imagine, there is no shortage of topics for conversation when Carol and I sip our morning coffee. We always awaken before dawn to get an early start on the day and give ourselves that relaxing alone-time to talk about whatever is going on that day or week—whether in our own lives or the world. We value these shared moments at our ranch in rural Pasco County, a place that has been a sanctuary for us for two decades, with its long, winding drive through acres of cattle land and clusters of oak, cypress, maple and palm trees. We love our house—a modern, open, Frank Lloyd Wright type of design created by an architect in town, Bruce Houghton. I'd seen some of the designs by his firm and it was clear that they weren't just a cookie-cutter style—and that's the reason I hired him. He asked me what kind of home I wanted, and I said, "Well, I'm an automobile dealer and I'll give you carte blanche to design my home. Tell me what you want for your architectural fee, and I'll pay that up front. And then you design my house.' "

But I did have a few requirements, starting with cypress wood on the outside and solid oak on the inside. We also wanted to take advantage of being in Florida and the hot, sunny days. It seemed to me that so many houses here don't do that. Our architect designed the roof with a 40-foot, glass square in the middle, covered by a six-foot overhang—creating protection from the sun while allowing in the light. With all the oak trees around the house, we get plenty of shade. Lastly, I asked that a design be created that allowed us to "live" in every room on any given day. I wanted to be able to walk through the house and enjoy the paintings we have on the wall, enjoy our antiques, enjoy our big library filled with countless books on myriad topics Carol and I, as avid readers, have devoured over the years.

This amazing place has been our home the past two decades, but soon we'll be saying goodbye to it. We're each 83 and the time has come to make a change, though I'm not talking about moving into assisted living or a senior neighborhood. We're building a brand new home an hour to the north in the serene, wooded countryside of Brooksville that has the familiar, rural feel of Arkansas and Oklahoma. Slowing down into quiet retirement isn't part of our plans just yet, even though the drive will be a little longer to catch the USF Bulls playing football on autumn Saturdays.

Carol and I plan to stay on the move with one project or another, and perhaps do a little more of the world travel that has been such an important part of our lives. Seeing the world has been an enriching, educational experience, especially our many personal trips with the worldwide travel company that coordinated our adventures. For the entire year leading up to departure dates, the group sent us books and literature about our particular destination, and also hired university professors to come along and offer lectures as we went. It was like a master's course in culture, politics and geography, teaching us so much about a country before we even set foot in it. And it was a wonderful way to satisfy our ongoing desire to keep learning and expanding our base of knowledge.

Some of our travel was purely for fun, like our trip to France in 1983 for my induction in the wine-tasting society known as La Confrérie Des Chevaliers Du Tastevin. They were initiating me at a manor house when Carol and I noticed a Standard Oil barge, with a handful of men stepping off—one of them was a friend, John Swearingen, the Chairman of the Board of Standard Oil in Indiana and it turned out we were both being initiated at the same time. It was a terrific evening, though our hosts spent much of the time speaking French and complaining about President François Mitterand. With such excellent wine to taste, it didn't matter that we had no idea what they were saying much of the night.

We've actually been to 120 countries, exceeding the 100 required by the Traveler's Century Club, and I've made a point of hitting a golf ball on every continent we have visited. About six years ago, there was still one last continent that beckoned— along with an opportunity to tee off in an exotic new land. When the chance arose to take a trip to Antarctica, it was too much to pass up. I'm not sure that Carol was as excited as I was over the prospect of visiting the frozen tundra down under. But she was a good sport, especially considering we'd already made reservations to go on a train trip across Russia—starting in Vladivostok and finishing in Moscow. "I was really looking forward to traveling across Siberia, but all of a sudden Frank decided he wanted to see Antarctica—so off we went," Carol remembers.

The way I saw it, Antarctica was the only continent we had never set foot on. With Carol's reluctant blessing, we changed plans and booked travel with a National Geographic crew. The itinerary required that we fly to Santiago, Chile, catch a bus to the southernmost tip of the country and join up with the crew there. They had a fleet of three or four ships and we boarded one of them, embarking on our voyage around Cape Horn through the fabled Drake Passage.

We remembered studying this dangerous route in high school geography, and it was worse than anything we'd ever read. Huge waves crashed steadily against our ship and the gusting wind howled non-stop. "We'd be eating breakfast and then we'd hit rough water and all the food would be in your lap," Carol recalls. That went on for four days, a challenging excursion to say the least. They strung ropes across the ship so you'd have something to hold onto and keep your balance when you were walking. Finally, we arrived at the first island and donned layers of warm clothing and rain suits to protect us from the sub-zero temperatures we'd soon encounter.

To reach our destination, we had to disembark from the ship and climb onto an inflatable vessel that would lead us to the land of snow and ice. Carol has a vivid memory of what awaited: "Someone asked, 'What do we do on this island?' and the tour guide answered, 'Well, you find a spot, sit down and watch the penguins.' True enough. For two hours, we watched the penguins. Then the guides came and got us and brought us back to the ship. We took off all our gear, had lunch and put all the gear back on and went back and did more penguin watching. We did this for five days. And there are a million, trillion penguins! We learned about all the different kinds, but that didn't really help. And let me tell you, it smelled to high heaven, because there were so many of them. You couldn't even see the snow."

All in all, we're both glad we could share the memory of another step in our long journey together. One of those steps, by the way, took us back to the Mayo Hotel in Tulsa about 10 years ago, after it had been sold to new owners and renovated. We had some business in the area and thought it would be fun to stay in the historic old hotel where we had gone to the prom as high school seniors. An idea occurred to me: this would be the perfect occasion to return the silver spoon that I'd taken that night in 1949 as a souvenir of our first date.

We pictured the reaction we'd get from the staff when we returned the spoon, engraved with the Mayo name, and explained its significance in our lives. But, as Carol remembers, it didn't work out that way. They couldn't have seemed less interested. "We were so disappointed! We thought they'd put a little story in the paper, but apparently our amazing spoon tale wasn't such a big deal after all—even though it always will be to us."

Throughout our marriage, Carol and I have always given each other strength and perspective, and that has especially been true during difficult times. And there was never a more trying experience than the pursuit of baseball and the tormenting bankruptcy that followed. We hung together through those rough, unrelenting seas, knowing we would make it through even stronger than ever.

We've had several friends who encountered harsh personal setbacks and wound up divorced or seriously depressed. We felt we just had to grab our bootstraps, pull them up and keeping on going. And we hope that sharing the story of our personal crisis may be of help to anybody being severely tested in life. You don't have to let a defeat knock you down, or keep you off your feet for long. I've thought a lot about this and we've both talked a lot about it as well. My business did not cause my problem. My financial pressure stemmed from baseball and the fact that I committed too much money to the quest. That was compounded when my partner, a very wealthy man, chose to decrease his participation. But there was something inside Carol and me that kept us going and moving to the next opportunity in life—or, as Carol quips, "Maybe we were just too dumb to know we were in trouble."

It certainly helped to have friends who stood by us. Bill Starkey, George Gage, Mike Urette and Earl Ware—those four men gave us unbelievable moral support and we are forever grateful to them for brightening up a dark period in our lives. As for baseball, Carol and I have moved past the emotional pain. It's in the past. But I did lose my appetite for Major League Baseball. I wish the Tampa Bay Rays and their organization well—I truly do—but I have never purchased a ticket or attended a big-league game since our pursuit of a franchise and the subsequent lawsuit. Nor do I plan to.

I will say that I very much appreciated the kind words of former St. Petersburg Assistant City Manager Rick Dodge, who had competed vigorously for a team against the Tampa Bay Baseball Group. Several years after the expansion Devil Rays were awarded to owner Vince Naimoli, Rick credited me with laying the groundwork for baseball coming to Tampa Bay. From the start, my whole intent was to try to enhance the community with a major league baseball team, and I do believe our efforts helped pave the way.

As I stated earlier, It would have been difficult to undertake as many projects as I did over the years without an absolutely top-notch staff working for me at my dealerships. That freed up more time for me to focus on other pursuits. And when it comes to new and interesting projects, my wife will tell you that I'm like a kid with a new toy. After I've taken something apart, re-assembled it and got it running well, I want another toy.

The pace in the car business has slowed for me in recent years. In the late 1990s, I sold off three dealerships comprising Precision Motorcars to Asbury Automotive in Orlando, and eventually sold my other dealerships to employees or family. But I couldn't stay out of the business completely, even though Carol made me promise. I recently purchased a Mitsubishi dealership and added a Mazda store. In addition, I stay busy every workday with my management company, Automotive Investments, visiting with members of my executive team, going over reports and keeping a hand in our various businesses, investments and projects.

One of those projects has tremendously exciting possibilities for the future: compressed natural gas, or CNG for short. The infrastructure for the potentially transformational product is still weak, but we are trying to help lead the way in this energy and cost-efficient gasoline for automobiles. In a nutshell, our business converts regular gas to CNG; for example, we just converted seven trucks for the City of Clearwater. Compressed natural gas equates to roughly 3,600 PSI, or pounds per square inch, and that requires a large, heavy-duty cylindrical tank. Furthermore, we convert the engine in such a way that it can operate either with regular gas or CNG, wherever it is available.

People are increasingly ordering pickup trucks with this dual-fuel setup—I just received a phone call from a man who wants to convert 250 trucks to natural gas. That remains a very expensive process but the result will be well worth it: filling up your tank at $1.25 a gallon rather than $3.50 a gallon and, down the road, making a significant difference in our daily lives and household budgets. Oddly enough, when I was a mechanic in 1955, we were converting trucks for natural gas, but that practice ended. At the time, none of the manufacturers were interested in pursuing it. But now, with the tremendous natural gas resources we have here in the United States, it's coming back with a vengeance and we are poised to take advantage of the opportunity.

It's been a tedious process, and I've pumped quite a lot of money into natural gas conversion the past several years. I've traveled all over Florida with two of my staff members, giving lectures from Miami to Pensacola. We're among the only ones doing CNG conversion in the state, and people are sending us trucks from Jacksonville, Apopka, Miami, Tallahassee, you name it. Manufacturers still don't want to deal with this, but they have at least begun making the conversion process easier. Engines are being manufactured now with something called "natural gas prep," which pre-wires and equips the engines for an easier changeover to CNG. That way we don't have to remove the intake manifold during conversion; we just have to add our system to the existing engines.

The next likely step in the evolution will involve the bulky 3,600 PSI tanks that need to be installed alongside the regular gas tank. The engineering departments at USF, the University of Texas and Northwestern University are collaborating on a type of metal that would eliminate the need for two gas tanks. A single new tank made of this special metal, which acts like a sponge, would simply release the type of gas that the engine utilizes. That could become a reality in the next three to five years. And if that happens, then you have genuinely changed the natural gas industry in America—and changed our energy for decades to come. That's what is so exciting about this endeavor.

I guess you could say I'm still keeping busy trying to figure out how things work and doing my best to fix them, characteristics that have the deepest of family roots. I think back to an application I once filled out to buy a dealership. One of the questions caused me to pause for a few moments: "Did your investment come from an inheritance?"

My initial reaction was to say no. But after some thought, I wrote, "My inheritance has been the substance of my privilege to be in business. I was fortunate to be born of loving and disciplined parents, who had the foresight to be unknowingly poor.

"My mother gave me love and understanding and an undying faith in God and mankind. My father provided the temper to the metal by demonstrating work ethic in an exemplary manner. As a welder on pipelines, he toured the country seeking any job that existed to provide the food and shelter for his family; while my mother provided the warmth and direction for our home. They performed their individual and invisible duties, with loyalty and devotion—to each other, to their children, and to God."

They are traits that I absorbed by osmosis, shaping the husband, father and businessman—and man—I am today. The gift my parents gave me was a sturdy foundation: a foundation for a life enriched by opportunity, adventure and a deep desire to make life better for my community and for the people who live in it. I hope you've enjoyed sharing this long road with me, from the dusty streets of Arkansas to the fast lane of the automotive world, as much as I've enjoyed having you along for the ride.

CLOSING THOUGHTS

One of the biggest mistakes people make as they traverse the challenges of life is constantly looking in the rear-view mirror.

I don't mean to suggest that we shouldn't look back on key decisions or events to review what happened or contemplate how we could have done something better or made a wiser decision. On the contrary, I believe it's essential that we learn from our mistakes. And I'm a big proponent of studying history to gain a better understanding of seismic events in the world. The more knowledge you have about events that have shaped our lives, the better off you'll be.

My point is that glancing in that rear-view mirror of your life too often can force you to take your eyes off the road ahead—and possibly miss out on opportunities in your path. If you're looking back too frequently, getting mired too much in the past, you're not going to have the vision necessary to move forward effectively.

My vision—the way I see the world around me, the way I view my dealings with people in business and everyday life—has always been shaped by a desire to act with integrity. There can be no better compass for any of us than to be guided by integrity, which, for me, is fueled by the core principles of honesty, compassion, fairness, hard work and ethical judgment. If you move forward living your life in keeping with your values, striving for integrity in the decisions you make and relationships with others, you will have gone a long way in building a foundation for success, regardless of the destination you've mapped out for your future.

The cornerstone of every business I've run has been built around the golden rule: Do unto others as you would have them do unto you. I don't think there is a better alternative to those words. I've always believed in treating customers with respect and courtesy and have rewarded my employees who mirror those traits.

There are no substitutes for integrity, honesty and credibility, nor should we ever compromise those principles. Whether we are dealing with employees or customers, with family, friends, or people we do not know—the golden rule should be a vital, integral part of our work and our daily lives.

Back in the days when I was employed by the Ford Motor Company, I worked for bosses who managed by fear and intimidation. I found that I achieved far better results managing by reward—giving my employees the room and independence to do their jobs, excel and achieve their potential, and rewarding them for jobs well done. As I wrote earlier, when employees feel that they are appreciated and respected, they will be happier and more likely to work to the best of their ability.

I know experienced professionals today who find themselves working for supervisors who micromanage them, or don't allow them to utilize their talents fully—that makes no sense to me, because everyone loses. By over-controlling, management fails to gain the full benefit of an employee's talents, and the employee feels stifled and unfulfilled—and more than likely will wind up looking for a new place to work.

As a business owner or department head, I've always believed that it was important to try to raise the management bar. We can raise the performance level of our managers by our own expectations of what they can achieve. When we set minimal goals, we tend to minimize peoples' real abilities. We can appoint committees and draw organizational charts until we're blue in the face, but unless we challenge our managers to be leaders, nothing will change or improve. When we do give our managers responsibility for getting things done, they often excel — and everyone wins.

I've challenged myself, meanwhile, to live as full and engaging a life as possible. Both Carol and I, as you know by now, continue to enrich ourselves through reading, traveling and constantly learning. We have found tremendous fulfillment in doing what we can to create opportunities for others to learn, thrive and pursue their dreams, and to enhance the community and region in which we live. My hope is that others, in a position to make a difference in the world, will consider how they can help—and then take meaningful action.

As I've grown older, I've learned many lessons. Chief among them is that the only constant in life is change. I understand the importance of keeping up with changes in technology, in culture and in society in general. Failing to do that, or simply refusing, is a recipe for getting left behind in a fast-changing world.

From a business perspective, the best example I can give you is the computer age that we're in: If you're not willing to learn and utilize the enormous amount of data that is produced electronically today, your business is going to suffer.

I've let you in already on a personal example of change: Carol and I are selling our ranch property and building a new, smaller house. My parents would never have considered doing that. But at our age, we think it's prudent to liquidate that asset, much as we love it, and simplify our lives. Change isn't always easy to accept but you must be ready to do it or be faced with potential difficulties—a truth that certainly applies to any business in today's changing economy.

I leave you now with some words from a speech I gave to University of South Florida students in 1982. I was talking to them about my keys to success, and my message holds just as true today as it did then.

"Many folks want to take a smooth and easy path to success, but that doesn't exist. Hard work, creativity, the ability to lead and a desire to excel are the key factors in success. There is no easy road."

And you can't get there by being fixated on your rearview mirror. Know what your vision is—and always let it guide you on your journey.

PHOTO GALLERY

LEFT: The house built of timber and sod in which my mother, Helen, was born outside of Bristow, Oklahoma in 1910. The family of eight lived inside this little home, beneath a roof packed with corn stalks and grass to protect it from the elements. It was a common type of dwelling in the rural, farm area.

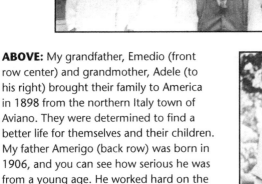

ABOVE: My grandfather, Emedio (front row center) and grandmother, Adele (to his right) brought their family to America in 1898 from the northern Italy town of Aviano. They were determined to find a better life for themselves and their children. My father Amerigo (back row) was born in 1906, and you can see how serious he was from a young age. He worked hard on the grape farm and never made it out of the sixth grade, but he was a smart, talented man who could build anything.

LEFT: My father and mother, Amerigo and Helen, were married in 1926. My mom ran the household, raising the children, while my father often left for long stretches to find work. He was a skillful laborer, nicknamed "Elmer" by his co-workers who couldn't pronounce Amerigo.

LEFT: Here I am (on the far left) with my brother, Paul, and sister, Patricia. We had fun as kids on the farm in Arkansas but also worked hard. I got my first job at age 9, shining shoes at a barbershop, and when we moved to Oklahoma, I delivered the Tulsa World and sold magazines door to door.

BELOW: I helped keep things running on the family farm in Oklahoma while my dad was away for long stretches working on the pipeline. This is our growing family around 1948, with my mom on the far left with little brother Timothy, along with Patricia, Paul and yours truly on the right.

ABOVE: Enjoying a family moment on the farm, with me (left), my sister Patricia and brother Paul, alongside our hard-working parents.

BELOW: Inside our farmhouse in Oklahoma during an early 1950s Christmas, relaxing at the dinner table with my father, me and Carol, Tim, Paul and my mom.

LEFT: Every pipeline contractor around wanted my dad on the job, and I occasionally got to join him after I turned 13 throughout my teenage years as a "welder's helper." This shot, in my later teens, was taken at the Arkansas River Crossing. The rigorous pipeline experience fueled my interest in learning how things were made.

ABOVE: When my father decided to buy a 260-acre farm, the job of running it fell to me for the eight months Dad was off working on pipelines. That included plenty of time on the tractor—one of my many duties that included running a bailing crew that included supervising about a dozen men. The young man in the middle we called Mo—an Oklahoma State student from Iran who went on to teach agriculture in the U.S.

RIGHT: After the United States was drawn into the Korean War in 1950, I enlisted in the Navy—on Oct. 24, 1950. I was assigned to a CV36 aircraft carried named the U.S.S. Antietam. This shot was taken in November 1952 in Nara, Japan, where I bought an arm-full of Christmas gifts to send home.

Frank L Morsani
Airman
United States Navy

I learned a lot about life—and management—during my Navy years fighting in the Korean War.

LEFT: I couldn't have been happier in 1950 to escort my pretty girlfriend Carol Walsh to her sorority's Chi Omega Spring Dance in our first year at Oklahoma State.

BELOW: We had a whirlwind wedding on Feb. 9, 1951 in Oklahoma, then hopped in our no-frills Buick and drove straight back to Hunter's Point in San Francisco to return to duty on the Antietam.

RIGHT: Our wonderful little girls, Leann and Suzy, savoring a little fishing in Floral City, Florida. Leann probably was enjoying the fact that she'd caught a fish and Suzy was still empty-handed.

BELOW LEFT: A favorite photo of Carol from early in our marriage.

BELOW: Fast-forwarding to a family portrait years later at the dedication of the USF medical center: Carol and I are joined by Leann with husband Mike Rowe (far right) and Suzy with husband Larry Anderson.

ABOVE: Receiving an award in the early 1990s as the first chairman of the Small Business Council of the U.S. Chamber of Commerce—a special moment I was glad to share with Carol.

ABOVE: A full-page ad in the *U.S. News & World Report* touting our Precision Auto Dealerships.

LEFT: Posing on the U.S. Chamber of Commerce's balcony, which has a terrific view of the White House and Washington Monument.

RIGHT: My work with the U.S. Chamber of Commerce was an unforgettable part of my life. It all began with my remarks officially accepting the role as the Chamber's Chairman of the Board in the mid-1980s.

BELOW: During my tenure with the U.S. Chamber, I escorted India's Prime Minister, Rajiv Gandhi during his visit to Washington, D.C.—one of many world leaders I hosted. Here I am handing Prime Minister Gandhi a box of tea—causing a moment of levity because tea is plentiful in India.

RIGHT: As President of the Tampa Bay Baseball Group, my efforts to help bring a Major League Baseball team to the Tampa Bay area ultimately proved to be an incredibly frustrating and costly experience, but I believe our work laid the groundwork for the eventual success of local efforts to land a team.

ABOVE: My work with the U.S. Chamber allowed Carol and me to get to know various U.S. Presidents and First Ladies. This shot with President Gerald Ford was taken in Tampa at a fundraiser at developer Al Austin's home prior to the 1976 election.

BELOW: Discussing business policy at a meeting in the White House with President Ronald Reagan. I spent a lot of time in Reagan's presence as well as members of his cabinet and officials from regulatory agencies. In meetings, I found him to be well prepared, very articulate and someone who knew what he was talking about.

ABOVE: At the U.S. Chamber of Commerce with a special visitor, President Reagan, marking my arrival as Chairman and Ed Donley's as Vice Chairman (Ed would eventually follow me as Chairman). In the center of the group is longtime Chamber president, Dr. Richard Lesher, who did a phenomenal job in his more than 20 years as head of the U.S. Chamber.

RIGHT: At the annual meeting of the Chamber in Washington, there would always be various events arranged for the wives. On this occasion, the itinerary included meeting First Lady Nancy Reagan at the White House, leading to this memorable moment for Carol in the mid-1980s.

LEFT: Greeting President George Bush at a Chamber-related function. I supported his run for president in 1980 and enjoyed working with him after he was elected in 1988.

RIGHT: Carol and I truly enjoyed our interactions with First Lady Barbara Bush. On this particular day, Carol and other wives of Chamber officials met Mrs. Bush at the White House. Carol remembers how Mrs. Bush learned early in the tour that one of her sons had spent the night in the Lincoln bedroom— so she sent word to him through an assistant that he better make the bed before we arrived to view the historic room.

LEFT: With U.S. Representative Mike Bilirakis from the 9th District of Florida and Bob Graham, who served Florida both as Governor and U.S. Senator.

ABOVE: An unforgettable experience during the trip Carol and I took to China while I served as U.S. Chamber of Commerce Chairman was a meeting with Chinese Premier Li Peng in 1988.

ABOVE: U.S. Representative Sam Gibbons, a 17-term Democrat, and I didn't always agree, but I respected him immensely—here he is introducing us at a party for friends we attended. With another politician I liked a great deal, U.S. Representative and former Secretary of Housing Jack Kemp.

BELOW: With my good friend, former Tampa Mayor and Florida Governor Bob Martinez. And sharing some fun with another friend, the late Tom McEwen, longtime sports editor and columnist for the *Tampa Tribune* (at a charity event involving Princess Anne that included *Lifestyles of the Rich and Famous* host Robin Leach).

LEFT: Carol and I have been deeply devoted to philanthropic work, from the arts to medicine to sports. A chance to be in the audience for the first-class Florida Orchestra was always good reason to smile.

VOLUME 3, ISSUE 4 · SUMMER 2005

LEGACY

Couple's Giving Comes From Life Lessons

INSIDE
» MAGNOLIA BALL HITS **HALF-MILLION DOLLAR MARK**
» **TINY GIVER** MAKES A DIFFERENCE
» GOLF TOURNAMENT HAS A **NEW SWING**

MOFFITT FOUNDATION

RIGHT: On the cover of *Legacy* magazine in story about our support of the amazing Moffitt Cancer Center in Tampa. Carol was active on Moffitt's Foundation board and we are proud to have supported the cutting-edge work done at the Moffitt Cancer Center.

FRANK AND CAROL MORSANI

LEFT: Carol served on the board of the Tampa Museum of Art in the late 1970s and early 1980s—and was on a committee that helped oversee construction of a beautiful new home for the museum.

Congratulations to Tampa Museum of Art on 25 years serving citizens of the Tampa metropolitan area. We also would like to applaud other institutions providing valuable service to this community and beyond. Moffitt Cancer Center and Research Institute, dedicated to the prevention and cure of cancer, strives toward excellence in patient care, research and education.

USF Health Science Center envisions combining medicine, nursing and public health education, so that doctors, nurses and public health professionals might learn together and thus collaborate to provide exceptional health care. Join us in celebrating art, science, medicine, and the spirit of giving.

CLOCKWISE FROM TOP LEFT: A night out at the downtown Tampa venue named for my wonderful wife, Carol Morsani—part of the Straz Center for the Performing Arts, and, at right, at a fundraiser for the Salvador Dali Museum in St. Petersburg. Below that, here I am with Colonel Joseph Ralston, who went on to become head of NATO. We've been honored to support higher education, including the university that made such a difference in our lives, Oklahoma State, where we've developed a close relationship with President Burns Hargis (at right)—and to each have received honorary doctorates. We're also very proud of the honorary doctorates bestowed by the University of South Florida, and we value our friendship with USF president Dr. Judy Genshaft and admire her remarkable leadership.

Frank, We started in 1993.
Thanks to you, football at U.S.F.
is a reality in 1995. Go Bulls.

Lee Roy
Selmon

ABOVE: One of my fondest memories has been working together with Lee Roy Selmon on the effort to bring football to the University of South Florida. This photo from the 1995 press conference announcing the news holds deep meaning to me. Lee Roy was such a caring, wonderful person and I'll always treasure our friendship.

LEFT: The rustic backyard view from our ranch home in Pasco County—a place that was like a sanctuary for us for more than two decades. We thank you for joining us on this journey through the pages of our lives.

NOTABLE CORRESPONDENCE

What follows are a handful of letters that have been written to or about me over the course of my career: from Presidents of the United States to local politicians to business people—and even to a former big-league owner whose note typifies the roadblocks we faced from Major League Baseball in our quest to land a team for Tampa Bay. It was hard to choose only six letters from so many years of correspondence, but these all hold great significance and meaning for me.

THE WHITE HOUSE

CONFERENCE ON SMALL BUSINESS

On behalf of President Carter, Conference
Director Michael Casey, and our complete
staff at the White House Conference on
Small Business, I am pleased to present
you with this Certificate of Appreciation.

We are most grateful for your part in
achieving a highly successful Conference
and in assuring the continued vitality of
America's small business community.

John Devereaux
Staff Director

March 1980

730 JACKSON PLACE, N.W.   WASHINGTON, D.C. 20006   202/456-7146

The Small Business Council was established soon after President Carter took office
and I was excited to become involved with it, working to create a favorable national
climate for the growth of small businesses.

Small Business Network

May 8, 1981

Mr. Bill Manck
Director, SBDC
University of South Florida
College of Business Administration
Center for Small Business Development
Tampa, Florida 33620

Dear Mr. Manck:

It would be difficult to overstate the contribution that Frank Morsani has made to Small Business in America through his leadership of the Council of Small Business of the U.S. Chamber of Commerce.

His special contributions starts with a willingness to devote himself to a cause he considers important. We are long past counting the hours he has spent or the miles he has traveled to work for small business in every part of the United States.

As a result, he may be more widely recognized across the country than in Tampa as a small business leader.

His contribution is composed also of a mixture of modesty and self-confidence with which he approaches life. On the one hand he instinctively treats the so called ordinary people around him with respect and consideration. He is just as quick to look a Cabinet Secretary or the President in the eye and say what he thinks.

What he thinks is merely always sound, while being practical about what individuals in groups can do to help small business.

What Frank Morsani has contributed most is that quality we call leadership, the rare capacity to transmit life and vitality into a group, to help members of the group develop a feeling of common purpose. Over the years he has gained the deep respect of his colleagues on the Chamber's Board of Directors and the loyalty of the members of the council.

Several of those council members helped in drafting this letter, and they join me in thanking those who organized the Small Business Week in Tampa for recognizing Frank Morsani. We wish we could join you in the events to express personally our love and respect.

Cordially,

Ivan C. Elmer
Director
Small Business Center

U.S. Chamber of Commerce
1615 H Street, N.W.
Washington D.C. 20062
(202) 659-6180

This letter about my work on behalf of small businesses in the country was sent from the U.S. Chamber of Commerce to Bill Manck, then the director of the Small Business Development Center at the University of South Florida. It meant a great deal to me.

THE WHITE HOUSE

WASHINGTON

July 29, 1985

Dear Frank:

Thank you very much for your kindness
and your prayers.

There is much to love in this land of ours,
but by far the most heartwarming of all is
people like you. You have given Nancy
and me the strength we needed during
these days.

God bless you, your colleagues and all the
members of the Chamber.

Sincerely,

Ronald Reagan

I admired President Reagan greatly and was proud to work with the President and
members of his administration during both of his terms. I was touched by the
graciousness of his words.

H. E. Chiles
P. O. Box 186
Fort Worth, Texas 76101

(817) 731-5250

August 25, 1988

Dear Frank:

Thank you so much for the many courtesies extended
to Weldon Aston, Bill Bogle and me while we were
in Tampa earlier this week.

You were very kind to arrange for the delightful
dinner at the hotel. Our accommodations there
were absolutely the finest, the food was marvelous,
and even more important, our visit ended on the
very positive note of accomplishing the results we
had worked toward over all these past weeks.

I feel a great relief, and I am sure you do too,
that all the legal fine points have at last been
handled, and we can move ahead to finalize our deal.

Thanks again for everything. I look forward to
seeing you again soon, and to working with you for
a smooth, efficient transfer of ownership.

Best personal regards.

Sincerely,

H. E. Chiles

This 1988 letter from then-Texas Rangers owner Eddie Chiles, following our dinner with him and several associates at a Tampa hotel, underscores the agreement they'd made to sell the franchise to me. It was typical of the deceit and dishonesty I experienced at the hands of Major League Baseball in our quest to bring baseball to the Tampa Bay area, as you read about in Chapter Nine.

GEORGE BUSH

January 5, 1993

Mr. F. L. Morsani
911 Leonard Rd.
Lutz, FL 33549

Dear Mr. Morsani,

This is a brief note to thank you for the friendship and
steadfast support you have given to me and my Administration
through your membership in the Republican Presidential Task Force.

Friends have always served as a source of inspiration and
strength in my life. Your support has been invaluable in our
efforts to keep America strong and free.

Over the past four years we have reduced the threat and
instability created by nuclear weapons, helped extend the
blessings of democracy abroad, opened foreign markets to our
nation's businesses, and repelled the aggression of a foreign
dictator.

We have worked to create the conditions in which
entrepreneurship will flourish, begun a renaissance in America's
schools, expanded our transportation system, enhanced our
nation's environment, made great strides in strengthening our
ability to compete internationally, and accomplished much in
improving the health and quality of life for all Americans.

Much good remains to be done, but we can look back with
pride on having set a course that will ensure a bright future for
our country and its people. We have sought to uphold the public
trust, and to build a better America -- a nation at peace, a
nation filled with opportunity, a prosperous America, and a good
America.

You have been with me in this important quest, and for that
I will forever be grateful. Thank you. God bless you, and God
bless the United States of America.

Sincerely,

George Bush

I was glad to have a chance to work with and support the efforts President George
H.W. Bush, who shared these kind sentiments as he prepared to leave office.

Pam Iorio, Mayor

January 30, 2006

Mr. Frank Morsani, President
Tampa Bay Performing Arts Center
1010 N. MacInness
Tampa, FL 33601-0518

Dear Frank:

It is a pleasure to join the Board of Trustees and staff of the Tampa Bay Performing Arts Center in saluting you for your leadership over the last several years. I know you have received numerous accolades for your many accomplishments but I wanted to make sure you know how much your dedication has meant to Tampa and its citizens.

As Chairman of the Board of Trustees, you have been instrumental in The Center's reputation as a leading arts facility dedicated to providing some of the highest quality programming and arts education programs in the nation. Under your tenure, The Center has continued to thrive, attracting more than 600,000 patrons to various events during the last year; and, with the addition of the Patel Conservatory, we can be assured the youth of our community will be free to explore their creativity and all The Center has to offer. Your efforts have played a major role in our goal of placing Tampa in the arts and cultural spotlight nationwide and you can be proud of what you have been able to achieve.

Although you will be stepping down as Chairman of the Board, I know that you will still have an active role in the future of both the Performing Arts Center and the City of Tampa because of your commitment to the concept of public service. Thank you again for all you do for our community.

Sincerely,

Pam Iorio

I derived great enjoyment and satisfaction from my work as Chairman of the Board of the Tampa Bay Performing Arts Center (now the Straz Center for the Performing Arts) and genuinely appreciated former Tampa mayor Pam Iorio's message as I stepped down from the job in 2006.

About Frank and Carol Morsani

"When I think of Frank Morsani, three things come to mind: strong family values, strong entrepreneurship and strong commitment to the community. Beyond his many dealerships, Frank was always very active in various organizations promoting business ethics and development. And one of the great aspects of both Frank and Carol is that they've shared their success with local institutions, whether it's the Straz Center for the Performing Arts, the University of South Florida or the University of Tampa—and now, the Morsani College of Medicine and USF Health Heart Institute being built in downtown Tampa. You can't drive around this community without seeing the footprint Frank and Carol have left."

— *Robert "Bob" Martinez, 40th Governor of Florida and past Mayor of Tampa.*

"Frank doesn't really want a lot of attention, even though he's had a lot of things named after him. He's a very humble, down-to-earth man and hasn't changed in that way. He has no class-consciousness at all. He feels comfortable with everybody and makes anyone he talks to feel welcome. He's obviously a very generous guy—and he's generous with his time as well as his money. He's one of the pioneers in the Tampa Bay area for charitable giving in a responsible manner. He also is a man with amazing confidence—he doesn't consider failure an option. He feels whatever he's involved in is going to be successful. Now, it hasn't always been for him, but he believes that nothing can knock him down. Adversity is just another challenge to him;

not anything that can defeat him. And Carol really keeps him grounded—she doesn't let him drift off into his own successes. She's a steadying force for him and a tremendous partner."

— Bill Starkey, former president of GTE

"Frank has a very self-deprecating sort of personality. That's what you see when you first meet him. Then you realize there are many layers to him. Among many fine attributes, he is very smart and observant. And I don't think there is a more genuine person than Carol. She is straight up all the way—you know exactly where you stand with her. There isn't an inauthentic cell in her body. She has that wonderful gleam in her eye and that little smile. They have been such a great team to be around."

— Judy Lisi, President and CEO of the David A. Straz, Jr. Center for the Performing Arts

"Frank and Carol are all about giving to good causes and not getting into the politics of it. They are the premier role models. They are giving without strings attached, giving for the cause of helping others. They enjoy doing that—and certainly we are grateful.

— Dr. Judy Genshaft, President, University of South Florida

"I was well aware of their success in business and their impact in philanthropy when I met them, but I think what took me aback is how enthusiastic they are about life. … And what I love is that Frank keeps making plans and buying businesses. Carol raises her eyebrows from time to time. But they have to do what keeps them going—and for Frank, it's making things happen."

— Burns Hargis, President, Oklahoma State University.

"Frank Morsani has to be among the true giants of philanthropy in our area, and for that matter within our state of Florida. His and Carol's contributions to not only higher education but also to numerous causes and projects that needed assistance are extremely significant. The Tampa Bay Area would not be as great an area as it is without their community leadership, involvement and support. Frank served on our Board of Counselors, the Board of Fellows and the Board of Trustees. The University of Tampa is very grateful for being able to count Frank and Carol Morsani among our most generous and loyal friends."

— *Dr. Ronald L. Vaughn, President, University of Tampa*

"You just feel the determination when you're around him. You understand that he's soft-spoken, but he's driven. He got elected as Chairman of the Board of the U.S. Chamber of Commerce by a board of CEOs from bigger companies. And he was able to lead them and persuade them on many important issues—even though basically he was a shy man in some ways. He has an inner confidence and a very agreeable personality that people warm up to right away. That helped him build consensus and accomplish many things."

— *Dr. Richard Lesher, former President of the U.S. Chamber of Commerce*

CPSIA information can be obtained at www.ICGtesting.com
Printed in the USA
LVOW01*1912220915

455299LV00003B/6/P

9 780692 525135